Women's Voices On The Pacific

Border // Culture

Maisonneuve Press

Women's Voices On The Pacific

The International Pacific Policy Congress

Edited and Compiled

by

Lenora Foerstel

Women for Mutual Security

Maisonneuve Press
Publications of the Institute for Advanced Cultural Studies
Washington, D.C., 1991

Lenora Foerstel, editor. *Women's Voices on the Pacific: The International Pacific Policy Congress*

© Copyright 1991 by Maisonneuve Press
P.O. Box 2980, Washington, D.C. 20013-2980

All rights reserved. Except for fair use with due citations, no part of this book may be reproduced without written permission from the publisher.

Maisonneuve Press is a division of the Institute for Advanced Cultural Studies, a non-profit collective of scholars concerned with the critical study of culture. Write to the Director for information about Institute programs.

Printed by BookCrafters, Fredricksburg, VA. Manufactured to meet the standards of the Committee on Production Guidelines for Book Longevity of the Council of Library Resources.

Photographs by Diana Sheridan, except where noted.

Library of Congress Cataloging-in-Publication Data

International Pacific Policy Congress (1991: Port-Vila, Vanuatu)
    Women's voices on the Pacific: the International Pacific Policy Congress ; edited and compiled by Lenora Foerstel for Women for Mutual Security.
    p. 156, vii   cm.
Congress held in Port-Vila, Vanatu, Jan. 6-12, 1991.
Includes bibliographical references
ISBN 0-944624-13-8 (cloth) :   ISBN 0-944624-14-6 (pbk.)
1. Women in politics—Pacific Area—Congresses.
2. Women and peace—Pacific Area—Congresses.
3. Security, International—Congresses. 4. Economic development—Environmental aspects—Congresses. 5. Nuclear weapons—Testing—Congresses.
I. Foerstel, Lenora, 1929 – . II. Women for Mutual Security. III. Title.
HQ1236.5.P16I57   1991   91-22452
305.42—dc20   CIP

Women for Mutual Security is an international coalition committed to world peace and common security. The goals of WMS are to develop women's leadership in world policy-making, assure women a voice in the formation of foreign policy, and lead the way to a new balance between disarmament and development.

Contents

Lenora Foerstel	1	History Of The Congress
Hettie Tinsely	15	A Letter To Lenora
Margareta Papandreou	21	International Women's Gulf Gulf Peace Initiative
Kuini Bavadra	36	Dictatorship In Fiji
Petite O. Peredo	43	United States Military Bases And Their Impact On Women In The Philippines
Susanna Ounei	57	The Plight Of The Kanak People In New Caledonia
Marilyn Waring	63	The System of National Accounts, Or The Measure And Mis-Measure Of Value And Production In Economic Theory
Rosalie Bertell	79	Survival, Not Economy, Is The Bottom Line
Marie-Thérèse Danielsson	87	Colonization In French Polynesia
Glenn Alcalay	93	Nuclear Colonialism in the Pacific
Leslie W. Scott and Diana B. Sheridan	103	Nuclear Neo-Colonialism In The Ocean Of Peace
Edna Ross	111	Lobbying For Progress On A Comprehensive Test Ban Treaty

Hilda Lini	115	Tropical Deforestation
Kaye Mundine and Leigh Bowden	119	Hidden From History: An Examination Of Racism Towards Aboriginal People
La Donna Harris and Jacquiline Wasilewski	125	Intercultural Collaboration In The Pacific
Lilia S. Velasquez and Juana Ventura	131	Mexican American Women Meet With South Pacific Women
Dorothy Buckland-Fuller	135	Australia In The Pacific: A Big Brother, A Stooge Of America, Or A Friend And Ally?

Appendix

Albert Gore	143	A Resolution Concerning Deforestation In Papua New Guinea
	151	List Of Participants

Acknowledgments

Women for Mutual Security would like to thank the following organizations and individuals for their contributions to the International Pacific Policy Congress: the World Council of Churches, and in particular Priscilla Padolina of the Women's Sub-Unity of the W.C.C.; the General Board of Global Ministries, and especially Elizabeth Calvin, Executive Secretary, Ministry of Women and Children; The Sunflower Foundation and Richard Parker who acted as our liaison. We also wish to extend our appreciation to Ruth Lechte, World YWCA Energy and Environment, for bringing WMS and the World Council of Churches together.

We thank Evelyn Seegers, Kimi Bond, Madleine Gilchrist, Marie Muir, and Jancis Long for their individual contributions. For bringing outstanding women leaders from Australia and New Zealand to our coalition, we would like to thank Mavis Robertson and the organizations she represents, the International Peace Bureau and the Australian Coalition for Disarmament and Peace.

For their gracious hospitality, cooperation, and participation in our Congress, we thank Hildi Lini, Member of the Port Vila Parliament, Pastor Allan Nafuki and his Excellency Fred Kalomoane Timakata, President of Vanuatu.

The success of our Congress depended on the talents of individuals. Pat Toms, President of the South West Branch of WILPF, provided valuable video coverage of the Congress. Diana Sheridan took the wonderful Congress photographs that appear in this book.

For their sensitive advice and direction, we thank Ambassador Renagi Lohia, Permanent Representative of Papua New Guinea to the United Nations, and Ambassador Robert Van Lierop, Permanent Mission of the Republic of Vanuatu to the United Nations.

To Mr. Paul Darcy and his staff at the Vanuatu Radisson Hotel, we extend our appreciation for their patience, cooperation, and excellence service. Thanks finally to Michael Johnson of Greenpeace for supplying maps and essential research. Finally, we are grateful to Robert Merrill of Maisonneuve Press for his advice on the organization and development of this book.

Northern Mariana Islands (U.S.)
Saipan
Guam (U.S.)
Agana
Wake Island (U.S.)
FEDERATED STATES OF MICRONESIA
Enewetak
Kwajalein
Majuro
Yap
Koror
Trust Terr. of the Pacific Islands [Palau] (U.S.)
Caroline Islands
Truk Islands
Pohnpei
Kolonia
Tarawa
Yaren
NAURU
Banaba
New Ireland
New Britain
Bougainville
New
PAPUA NEW GUINEA
Port Moresby
Honiara
SOLOMON ISLANDS
Santa Cruz Islands
Ashmore and Cartier Islands (AUSTRALIA)
Darwin
Wyndham
Daly Waters
Cairns
Tennant Creek
Townsville
Mount Isa
Dampier
Coral Sea Islands (AUSTRALIA)
Port-Vila
VANUATU
New Caledonia (FRANCE)
Nouméa
Tropic of Capricorn
Rockhampton
Alice Springs
AUSTRALIA
Quilpie
Brisbane
Geraldton
Kingston
Norfolk Island (AUSTRALIA)
Kalgoorlie
Perth
Broken Hill
Darling
Lord Howe Island
Esperance
Whyalla
Sydney
Albany
Adelaide
Murray
Canberra
Melbourne
NEW ZEALAND
Launceston
Hobart
Tasmania
Greymouth
Invercargill
Stewart Island

Midway Islands
(U.S.)

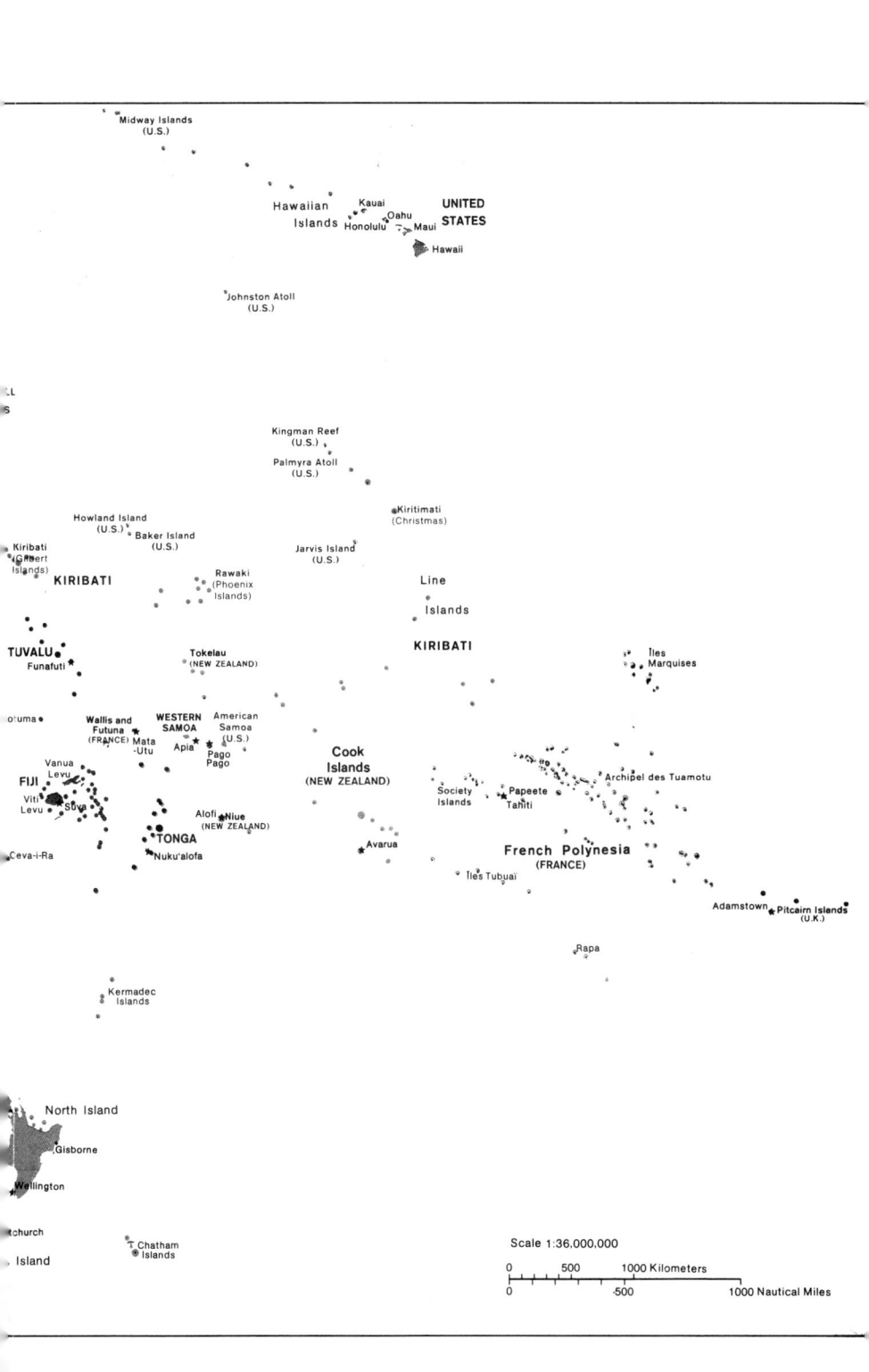

Hawaiian Islands
Kauai
Honolulu Oahu
Maui
Hawaii

UNITED STATES

Johnston Atoll
(U.S.)

Kingman Reef
(U.S.)
Palmyra Atoll
(U.S.)

Kiritimati
(Christmas)

Kiribati
(Gilbert Islands)

KIRIBATI

Howland Island
(U.S.)
Baker Island
(U.S.)

Rawaki
(Phoenix Islands)

Jarvis Island
(U.S.)

Line Islands

KIRIBATI

Îles Marquises

TUVALU
Funafuti

Tokelau
(NEW ZEALAND)

otuma

Wallis and Futuna
(FRANCE)
Mata-Utu

WESTERN SAMOA
Apia

American Samoa
(U.S.)
Pago Pago

Cook Islands
(NEW ZEALAND)

Society Islands
Papeete
Tahiti

Archipel des Tuamotu

Vanua Levu
FIJI
Viti Levu
Suva

Alofi Niue
(NEW ZEALAND)

TONGA
Nuku'alofa

Avarua

French Polynesia
(FRANCE)

Îles Tubuai

Ceva-i-Ra

Adamstown Pitcairn Islands
(U.K.)

Rapa

Kermadec Islands

North Island
Gisborne
Wellington

churchh
Island

Chatham Islands

Scale 1:36,000,000

0 500 1000 Kilometers
0 500 1000 Nautical Miles

Top – Lenora Foerstel and His Excellency Fred Kalomoane Timakata, President of Vanuatu. *Bottom* – The Congress was well attended by residents of Vanuatu, especially women.

History Of The Congress

Lenora Foerstel

The concept for an International Pacific Policy Congress emerged in June of 1988, when an international delegation of women arrived at the Moscow Summit where U.S. President Ronald Reagan and Soviet President Mikhail Gorbachev met to sign formally an agreement between the two nations for a reduction in their nuclear weapons stockpiles and missile systems. While in Moscow, this group—Women for Mutual Security—urged a comprehensive test ban treaty leading toward the abolition of nuclear weapons and an international commitment to respect the sovereignty of Third World nations. As the governments of the Soviet Union and United States negotiated new treaties, it became painfully clear that the proliferation of Western military bases in the Third World would not be challenged in this dialogue.

Lenora Foerstel teaches cultural history at the Maryland Institute, College of Art in Baltimore. Her career research on the South Pacific began with extended field work with Dr. Margaret Mead in Papua New Guinea. She has written numerous articles, produced several films, and recently co-authored a book, *Confronting the Margaret Mead Legacy: Scholarship, Empire, and the South Pacific* (Temple University Press). Foerstel is the North American Coordinator for Women for Mutual Security and has served as a delegate to the First International Conference on Women, Peace, and the Environment held in Moscow in 1989. More recently she coordinated and convened the 1991 International Pacific Policy Congress in Vanuatu.

Nations like the Pacific Island States would remain under *de facto* American military control. Throughout the Pacific, the United States commands hundreds of military bases which threaten the economic and social security of Pacific people. Between 1947 and 1957, the United States tested twenty-three atomic bombs on Bikini Atoll and forty-three atom bombs in Enewetak. By the year 1985, Pacific Island nations served as testing grounds for twenty-one British, one hundred-six American, and one hundred-fifteen French atomic and hydrogen bombs.

At a U.S. / Soviet press conference held for the international visitors in Moscow, one woman asked why the Pacific nations, riddled with military bases and strategic weapons, were not represented at the Summit. The question was ignored by politicians and press alike, but several of the visiting women decided it was time to organize an International Pacific Congress to address this issue and increase public awareness of the growing military threats to Pacific people.

The proposed Congress was initially planned for Papua New Guinea which, like Fiji, was regarded as a leader in the Nuclear-Free and Independent Pacific movement. However, the United States had already earmarked Fiji and Papua New Guinea as key regional states for further militarization. A year earlier, on May 14, 1987, a military coup occurred in Fiji. It was later revealed by the present Prime Minister of Fiji, Ratu Mara, that U.S. Secretary of State George Shultz had "given his blessings to the post-coup provincial government, and that the U.S. was on standby to help if needed" (Watts and James, 1987). Members of Fiji's ousted government have expressed the belief that the U.S. was directly involved in the overthrow of the Labour Government of Timoci Bavadra.

One of the first policies carried out by Fiji's new military government, headed by Prime Minister Ratu Mara, was to declare it a crime to print, publish, or circulate documents opposing any orders given by the new administration. Indeed, an easy victim of the coup was journalist Jole Moala, the associate editor of Fiji's independent daily newspaper, the *Fiji Sun*. The May, 1988 issue of *Island Business* states, "The detention of the *Sun* journalist is among 20 examples of attacks on the Fiji press last year . . ." (Lomas, 1988). Besides the closure of the *Fiji Sun* and *Fiji Times*, there was frequent "censorship of radio news, detention of publishers, arrests, and expulsion of foreign journalists, seizure of their films and attempts to censor their reports" (Lomas, 1988).

On October 19, 1988, Michael Somare, the First Prime Minister of Papua New Guinea, met with American Secretary of State George Shultz and Secretary of Defense Frank Carlucci to discuss a bilateral agreement on defense and security. It was decided that the U.S. would send military advisors to Papua New Guinea to train a small army and there was preliminary discussion on establishing an American military base on the Island of Manus in the area of Lombrum and Momoti. This new military partnership made it clear that the U.S. regarded Papua New Guinea—like Fiji—as another nation to be weaned away from the nuclear-free movement. The United States and France began pouring large sums of money into Papua New Guinea and Fiji while refusing to sign two major international treaties which would have prohibited nuclear weapons in the region as well as nuclear testing and dumping of nuclear waste.

The Israeli presence in the South Pacific, including sales of the advanced military aircraft to Papua New Guinea, demonstrates still another form of militarization: the escalation of "Low Intensity Conflict" in the region. The major goal of "Low Intensity Conflict" is to prevent Third World nations from controlling their own economies and forming cooperative regional networks free from Western influences. As village people learn more and more about their rights, they organize and express their frustrations through new political structures. The U.S. and France, therefore, foster low intensity wars with surrogate armies or insurrectionary groups focused against the increasingly radicalized Pacific people, as was the case in Fiji and the Bougainville crisis.

Despite their concerns over the political directions taken by the Papua New Guinea government, a delegation of women traveled to Port Moresby to negotiate arrangements for a South Pacific Congress in that country. The women met with Robbie Namaliu, Prime Minister of Papua New Guinea, Michael Somare, now Minister of Foreign Affairs, and William Dihm, Secretary of Foreign Affairs. All three officials expressed enthusiasm for the Pacific Congress, stating that this would be the first international congress ever held in their country. All of the meetings were attended by Bungtaba Brown who was at the time President of the National Council of Women of Papua New Guinea and her delegation. The National Council of Women is striving to change the repressive conditions facing women in Papua New Guinea.

The women's organizations of Papua New Guinea are extremely active and totally involved in community development, but their work is primarily voluntary. They receive no formal training or funding. Women in Papua New Guinea remain subject to male dominance, and those who question the authority of their husbands are often beaten. Seventy-three percent of the women murdered in Papua New Guinea are killed by their husbands.

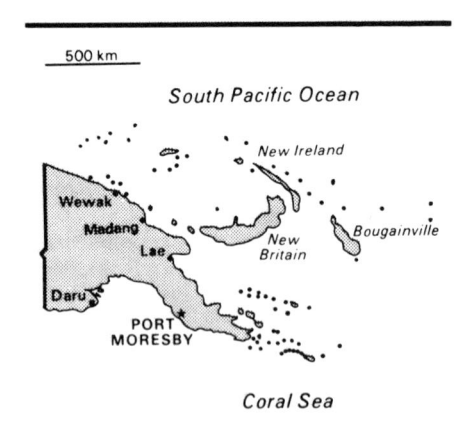

Papua New Guinea
Parliamentary democracy, independent since 1975. Population, 3,822,876 mostly Melanesian. Total area, 461,690 km^2.

A few months after our visit to Papua New Guinea, the Bougainville crisis broke out. Villagers and landowners began to rebel, rejecting the unsolicited introduction of western mining companies in their region. The villagers had decided to rid their land of the mining giant, Conzin Riotinto which had already gouged a pit some 400 meters deep and covering several square miles. The extensive pollution created by the mining destroyed the local farm land, forcing many people to become squatters on their own land. Negotiations were attempted, but despite the fact that Bougainville is a matriarchal society, the women were largely ignored in the process. The government of Papua New Guinea, eager for corporate taxes, continued to encourage foreign investors like Conzin Riotinto of Australia, whose profits are removed from the country. The villagers and local landowners whose land and labor are used to develop the mining industry, receive only subsistence compensation from the mining companies. Eventually, these inequities led the people of Bougainville to rebellion and secession from Papua New Guinea. The Papua New Guinea government responded with military force to crush the Bougainville rebels and the conflict escalated.

Women for Mutual Security was soon informed that due to the hostilities in Bougainville the Papua New Guinea government could no longer guarantee the safety of the women who would attend the proposed Congress. Initially it appeared that the Congress might be permanently canceled, but an alternative location on the island nation of Vanuatu was proposed. In July 1990, the WMS Coordinator for the Congress met with Ambassador Renagi Lohia, Permanent Representative of Papua New Guinea to the United Nations and followed up this meeting with Ambassador Robert Van Lierop, Permanent Mission of the Republic of Vanuatu to the United Nations. These meetings confirmed WMS's feelings that Vanuatu was the place to hold its Congress. Vanuatu—formerly the New Hebrides—is a prominent supporter of a nuclear-free and independent Pacific and a champion of liberation for New Caledonia, East Timor, West Papua, and Tahiti. The Vanuatu government had the courage to ban two American warships from its territorial waters when the U.S. Navy refused to reveal whether or not the ships were armed with nuclear weapons.

In August 1990, the WMS Coordinator went to Vanuatu to negotiate the Congress. At the time, no one could have anticipated the scale of the imminent hostilities in the Persian Gulf. The U.S. would soon be conducting the most intensive bombing campaign in human

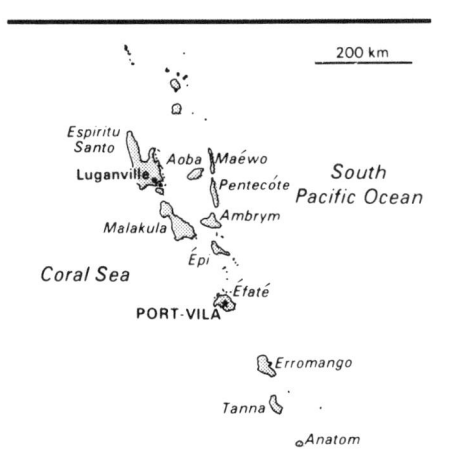

Vanuatu
Independent republic since 1980 (formerly New Hebrides). Population, 165,006: 94% Melanesian, 4% French. Total Area, 14,760 km².

history, reducing with space-age weapons a relatively advanced Third World nation back to "a preindustrial society"—as it was phrased by a panel of United Nations observers after the bombing ceased. Just two weeks before the WMS Congress was to convene, in December 1990, Margarita Papandreou, Global Network Coordinator, faxed a message to Lenora Foerstel stating that WMS would have to divide its energies, sending one group to the Pacific Congress while organizing another group to meet in Baghdad. WMS formed the International Women's Gulf Peace Initiative and brought a delegation to Baghdad on January 7, 1991 to meet with their counterpart, the Executive Board of the General Federation of Iraqi Women (see the statement by Margarita Papandreou in this volume).

Women around the world initiated proposals and formed actions committees with the hope of preventing the Gulf War. Some joined the Gulf Peace Camp, made up of citizens from many nations. They set up camps on the Iraq/Kuwait border, serving as human barriers to war. Others boarded the Peace Ship to bring food and medicine to the women and children of Iraq who were suffering desperate shortages caused by the sanctions imposed on their nation. The Peace Ship carried some 240 passengers, most of them women from ten Arab countries, the United States, Japan, Italy, and China. Among the women was Faye Williams, a former candidate for Congress from Louisiana and now Staff Counsel to U.S. Representative Mervyn Dymally (Dem.-California).

The ship set off on December 5th and stopped at ports along the Mediterranean and Red Seas, taking on a cargo of food and medicine to deliver to the people of Iraq. When the ship reached the Arabian Sea, it was intercepted by American and Allied warships. Faye Williams described the brutal event: "The Marines boarded the ship, beating back the women, shouting foul language and shooting guns over our heads. Many of the women were injured. The attack lasted about ten hours. Many of the young Marines came to the ship in Rambo or John Wayne style. They beat and kicked the women. While we were aware that the ship might be stopped, never in our wildest imagination did we think that we were going to be victims of a full scale military attack." The ship was delayed for two weeks while U.S. officials forced the removal of sugar, cooking oil, spagetti, and rice. Finally on January 14th the ship was allowed to dock at Basra. From there, some women hurried to Baghdad and all soon departed Iraq for their own countries, barely missing the first American air attacks. In spite of the women's efforts, the American blockade succeeded in keeping the supplies of food and medicine from reaching the people of Iraq even though humanitarian assistance of this sort was not prohibited by the United Nations resolution; it was merely U.S. policy or Bush's personal interpretation of the UN resolution. Williams says she believes that the ship was one of the first targets bombed as it sat in port at Basra before its cargo could be unloaded.

Petite Peredo, Secretary General of GABRIELA (General Assembly Binding Women for Reform, Integrity, Equality, Leadership, and Action) originally planned to join the women at the Pacific Congress as one of the key speakers but was called back to the Philippines. Members of GABRIELA feared that the Gulf War would affect their country, given the major American military bases in the Philippines. The lecture she was not able to deliver in person to the Congress is published here for the record.

In all forty women from eleven different countries arrived at Port Vila, Vanuatu, on January 7, 1991, to participate in the International Pacific Policy Congress. Among the South Pacific leaders who attended were Kuini Bavadra, Head of the Labour and Coalition Party in Fiji; Amelia Rokotiuvuna, a Fijian activist; Susanna Ounei, Presidente Du Groupe des Femmes Kanak en Lutte; Josephine Abaijah and Louise Aitsi, political activists for Paupua New Guinea Women; Ngaire Tehira, a Maori activist; Fanaura Kingstone from the Cook Island and Social Development Advisor in the Pacific; Kay Mundine, Aboriginal activist; and Hilda Lini, Member of Parliament from Port Vila, Vanuatu.

Among the prominent European women attending the Congress were Rosalie Bertell, author of *No Immediate Danger*; Marie Thérèse Danielsson, co-author of *Poisoned Reign*; Marilyn Waring, author of *If Women Counted*; Marvis Robertson, Vice President of the International Peace Bureau and Convener of the Australian Coalition for Disarmament and Peace; Jean McLean, Member of Parliament,

Victoria, Australia; Marie Muir, National President of the Union of Australian Women; Ann Symonds, Parliament House, Sydney, Australia; and Joyce Clark, National Director for the Australian Peace Committee. Among the many leading American women was La Donna Harris, President of Americans for Indian Opportunity and Madeline Duckles, editor, Berkeley Newsletter of Women's Strike for Peace. The Congress participants met in sessions to hear the presentation of research and in informal workshops where ideas were shared and issues debated. Perhaps the most valuable part of the Congress was the casual interchanges between women of so many different cultural backgrounds. We soon discovered how much women all over the world share in their concerns for the problems of communal and environmental degradation.

Kuini Bavadra, a keynote speaker, described the illegal overthrow of Fiji's coalition government and its 1970 Independence Constitution. "The Coalition came to power in 1987 on the strength of a comprehensive program of social reform intended to improve the living standards of ordinary working people irrespective of their race or creed." Ms. Bavadra related world events, including the Gulf War, to the problems in her country.

Susanna Ounei, leader of the FLNKS (Front de Libération National Kanak et Socialiste), described the effects of French colonialism on New Caledonia and her people's struggle for independence. The 1988 "Matignon Accord," signed by the French Government and the FLNKS leaders, has not reduced the political repression suffered by the Kanak people. Ms. Ounei asked the Pacific Congress to prepare a resolution asking that New Caledonia be given priority on the United Nation's decolonization list.

Josephine Abaijah, Head of the Port Moresby City Council, and Louise Aitsi, a political activist, expressed their concern over the sharp increase in violence against women in Papua New Guinea (PNG). The major issues causing the violence are rooted in vast unemployment and a lack of programs for basic human needs. Law and order break down when people cannot find jobs. "Every year thousands of young men leave the villages seeking work. With PNG's new foreign educational system, the young people seek a new materialist world,

Vanuatu women in an open-air market.

one which is enhanced by Western TV and video tapes." Ms. Aitsi accused her government of placing little value on good roads, clean water, health care and education. Foreign aid to Papua New Guinea, she said, never reaches the people. She concluded, "Women hold the key to the solution to their problems. If women were given full participation in national life, and in the mainstream economy of their nation, they would turn their country around."

Amelia Rokotiuvuna noted that Fijian women have faced increasing violence since the Fijian coup and she concluded, "The politics of rape and violence have a lot to do with social breakdown."

The effects of Western economic power on Pacific people include social dislocation, fractured communities, broken morals and resultant increases in robbery, rape, and murder. Mining and deforestation by Western companies has affected both the livelihood and the environment of Pacific nations. Some 3.2 million tons of waste have been dumped into the Third World, with the Pacific among the major recipients. Toxic and carcinogenic chemicals in the waste leach into the land and waters, threatening local agriculture and fishing and eventually threatening the health of the people.

During the Congress, Pacific women portrayed the vulnerability of their small island nations, while the Europeans women drew parallels with the policies of the industrialized world in other nations around the world. Rosalie Bertell described the adverse effects of radiation and chemical wastes on human health and reproduction. Like Louise Aitsi, Rosalie stressed the need for the inclusion of women and a feminist perspective in the decision-making centers of society.

In her address to the Pacific Congress, Marilyn Waring, a leading feminist economist, emphasized the misuse and misrepresentation of women in national economic analyses and statistics recognized by organizations such as the United Nations and the World Bank. The work of women is relegated to a hidden economy which is never measured by governments, financial institutions, or corporations. The economic statistics prepared by the world community are part of a system which attributes "little or no value to peace, pays no heed to the preservation of national resources or to the labour of the majority of its inhabitants, or to the unpaid work of the reproduction of human life itself, not to mention its maintenance and care." Ms. Waring concluded that until the activities of women acquire social significance and political influence, there will be no improvement in the quality of life for the vast majority of the world's people.

Hilda Lini, a key figure at the Congress, said the participants had gained a greater awareness of and sensitivity to the cultural heritage of Pacific peoples. They had the opportunity to examine the political, social, and economic problems of women from the Pacific and around the world. The participants at the Congress will continue to serve as a network for women's groups in support of the Third World people and their ecology.

References

Lomas, Peter. (May, 1988). "Pressure on the Inquiring Fiji Journalists," *Island Business*, p. 20.

Watts, Max and James Mark. (November, 1987), "A Coup in Question," *Covert Action Information Bulletin*, p. 7.

What Is Women For Mutual Security?

Margarita Papandreou
Global Coordinator

Women for Mutual Security had its origin in the United States as an *ad hoc* committee formed rather hurriedly to take a group of women to Geneva at the time of the first Summit meeting between Soviet President Mikhail Gorbachev and U.S. President Ronald Reagan in 1985. The group called itself "Women for a Meaningful Summit," and its purpose was more that of a watchdog—that is, the women would be there to shout, if necessary, and to insist that decisions were "meaningful" or significant. It was a period of time when the nuclear threat and the stockpiling of more and more nuclear weapons were creating anxiety all over the world. Perhaps "fear" is a better word. That group was able to meet with Gorbachev, but not with Reagan, in spite of efforts to do so.

At our first organizational meeting in Athens in 1986, we determined the goals of our network, what our strategies would be, and the kind of organizational structure we would adopt. We divided the world into seven regions and named three co-ordinators for each region with the co-coordinating for all regions being done out of an office in Greece. Margarita Papandreou was named the international co-ordinator. Each region was to be equal with the others with no hierarchical differences. We would work as a loose coalition, ideas could be proposed from any region, projects would be decided upon according to their timeliness and consistency with our goals. Another assembly meeting would be held after a five year period. Our goal was to de-militarize international relations. Our tactics were to confront the defense and political decision makers on nuclear weapons and challenge militaristic solutions to conflict in general. As we said, we wanted "women's voices to be heard in the corridors of power."

We worked together—women of the world—for a common cause and became convinced of the importance of social movements that are outside government. These citizen initiatives are somehow made for women. We can speak honestly and openly, we can use our creativity and originality, we can express values that are not often expressed in the public sphere and we can demonstrate our capacity to work together in a harmonious manner. We also prepare ourselves for participation in official politics in the future.

Soon it became apparent that our original title, "Women for a Meaningful Summit," was too narrow for the broader goals that we were all interested in. We felt that environmental issues, human rights (including those of children), questions of common security, and the problems of new institutions for conflict resolution were issues we all wanted to get involved in—and make an impact on. The coordination office in Athens decided to ask the members if they would agree to change the name to Women for Mutual Security in order to expand our focus. This was overwhelmingly accepted by all of the participants with the exception of the U.S. contingent.

Since the beginning we have carried out the following actions:

The International Assembly of Women, Athens, Greece, November 1986.

The Women's Defense Dialog with NATO, Brussels, June 1987, under the auspices of WMS and NATO Alerts Network, when women from fourteen countries met with NATO ambassadors and with Lord Carrington.

Congressional Hearings, Washington, DC, December 1987, under the auspices of WMS when women from twelve countries gave evidence to US Congressmen on the occasion of signing the INF Treaty.

The Warsaw Pact Women's Dialog, Sofia, Bulgaria, March 1988, under the auspices of WMS, and NATO Alerts Network, when women leaders from the East and West met with the foreign ministers of all Warsaw Pack countries.

Women Leaders and the NATO Defense Ministers Meeting, Brussels, April 1988 under the auspices of WMS, NATO Alerts Network, and Oxford Research Group, when women form seven NATO nations met with their defense ministers.

The Women's Summit, Greece, April/May 1988, under the auspices of WMS and attended by women leaders from the US and USSR and resource people form nine other countries. They produced a Peace Platform which was presented to the Soviet Foreign Minister and the US Assistant Secretary of State in Moscow in June 1988.

Women Leaders at Moscow Summit, Moscow, June 1988, under the Auspices of WMS when the women met with Raisa Gorbachev, Mikhail Gorbachev and with Rozanne Ridgeway from the US State Department and with Soviet General Nikolai Chervov.

NATO and Warsaw Pact Women, in Brussels, December, 1988.

Environment and International Security, in Athens, April 21-24, 1989, formulation by representatives of fifteen countries and W.I.D.F. and UNIDO of a women's environmental platform for use by governments and political activists.

Women's International Gulf Peace Initiative, January 7-11, 1991, under the auspices of WMS a delegation of seven women journeyed to Baghdad, Iraq, to meet with the Federation of Iraqi Women to attempt to work out a plan for averting war.

International Pacific Policy Congress, Vanuatu, January 6-12, 1991.

Women for Mutual Security
Athanasiou Diakou 29
GR. 146 71
Nea Erithrea, Greece

Dear Lenora,

As we discussed, here is a personal response to the Congress. It is very different in form from an information-oriented article I hope to construct for people in South Australia. Novice that I am, I cannot respond in depth to the issues raised and must leave that to the experienced contributors who opened up our thinking so powerfully and professionally.

Thank you for giving me the opportunity to attend. I shall never forget the close emotional bonds engendered by a common cause. Best wishes for peace in 1991.

I have been sitting in the darkness of our balcony watching tiny bats catch moths around the street lamp. They are masters of acrobatics, deft and neat, at one moment thrown in sudden detail by the light, then disappearing into the shadow. What a benevolent god they must thank for assembling the moths so conveniently each evening!

Above us a brilliant tropical sky wheels silently on, stars blazing through an unpolluted sky. It is mango season and the air is subtly perfumed with a sweetness as the fruit ripens and decays. Every experience and sensation at this time of year is touched by that smell so that when the season returns it will evoke scenes, moods and thoughts that I shared during the Congress.

Vanuatu seems a world away from the problems confronted during the week. But it is not. Just as easily as the airwaves bring us reports of what is happening in the Gulf war, does the same air carry evidence of our spoliation of the planet, and Vanuatu is as vulnerable as anywhere else on earth.

I have a sense of loss now that the group has dispersed. Some powerful emotions bound us together for a brief time; I have a picture of the physical tension of the inward-facing circle, the concentration

Perhaps the most important part of the Congress was the informal exchanges and the beginnings of international networks of women. (*L - R*) Diana Sheridan, Hettie Tinsley, Marie Muir, Josephine Abaijah, and Ann Symonds.

on issues raised. Now we are decentered and each of us has carried different messages away. My personal challenge is to recognize what I have learned so that I can raise the awareness of others, particularly in Australia.

It is certainly not expertise. I stand in awe of people like Rosalie, Marie-Thérèsa, and John—focusing their talents and honed skills on an area that has become their life's work. They are able to look at their achievements and say: "I did *this* and *that* was made to change for the better of the world."

Certainly not courage. I was humbled by the women who fight for freedom and justice every day of their lives, often at great personal risk. Kuini, Amelia, Josephine, and Susanna return to the "front line" while I will join the watchers in safety, assured of society's protection.

Not experience. How can I know the bewilderment of Kaye's aboriginal childhood, the fears of Fanaura's beaten wives, and the anguished knowledge behind Rosalie's meticulous data, tabling the suffering of innocent people.

It would be nice to claim that at least I cheered up a few hurting companions, but I didn't. That was achieved superbly by Ngaire, Dorothy and La Donna who take honours in hugs, love and T'ai chi. So what am I left with? What can I do?

I've decided I'm going to talk. They say women are good at it. I'll talk to anyone who'll listen but particularly to those who won't. I intend introducing controversial issues at polite dinner parties, bizarre agenda items at meetings where everyone hoped to fall asleep, and I'll be answering some of the questions to which I've never had answers before. Even better, when I respond to the fears of my students I'll carry a message of hope that there is a global network in action for a safer, fairer world and I have the addresses to prove it.

I intend challenging more often than I accept. I'll write to people who claim to represent me and ask what they're doing about the things I care about. And I'll make the effort to find out more about them myself. I know it's hard to move forward in commitment when you feel your daily round is challenging enough. Thank goodness, though, it is impossible to go back once your awareness has been raised—a point Eve accepted with far more alacrity than Adam!

I'm going to talk. There! I've begun already.

Hettie Tinsley

New Australian, Dreaming — Poem for Kaye Mundine

hettie tinsley, jan. 1991

I am an adopted child.
I have many sisters, many brothers,
Many colours.
I sing with my sisters under a blue sky
As we prepare fruits warmed by the sun.
I laugh with my brothers as we chase
Through the shadows by the river.
But it is from my mother and father
That I learn.
I learn to love who I am
For they show me who I am not.
They know where I come from
And I do not.

My mother is the colour of the creekbed
stirred up by the yabby net.
My father red, as the dust that twists
Above the mulga and settles like a breath
Across the land.
If I do not listen to my father and mother
I shall not know who I am.
The land that breathes through them
Will not speak to me
Nor to my brothers and sisters
If we do not listen.

So I sit quietly in the fire light
At night, when the jobs are finished
And the meals eaten.
While the stars catch fire overhead
I listen.
And my mother and father give me a shining gift
In the dark.
They let me love them.

Poem for women's voices

hettie tinsley, jan. 1991

Ladies, come to order. This meeting should have started ten minutes ago. We are wasting time.

> we do not measure time as clocks measure time we
> feel the pulse of time in the rhythms of our bodies
> in the course of our blood flow as our liquids surge
> and pull to the moon's time

That's all very well, but we shall never have this meeting if we use that criterion. We are wasting time.

> we waste time not lives
>
> we do not kill time as men do time kills us
> measuring out our lives in the cycles of a washing
> machine instead of the cycles of our land

They will say we are inefficient.

> they are right we are hopeless in destruction we
> cannot even kill time on the contrary we live many
> life-times in our own span we move in and out of the
> shadows of the images we are given carrying the
> small wedge of darkness that virginia woolf found in
> the garden
>
> man made time cannot fix us like a tie pin

Then we shall fail. We shall never get started. We are running out of time.

> time ran out on us our history was written out of
> time in manu-fractured books our time was no time at all

time abandoned us to tell the story of those who
fought wars

instead of those who gathered up the limbs on the
battlefields

time abandoned us to tell the story of those who
conquered

instead of those who bled from the wounds of rape

time abandoned us to tell the story of their
painters composers and scientists

instead of our farmers healers weavers and needle
workers

Well, that's it. We've run out of time and we've achieved nothing.

at last achieving nothing in quick time we destroy
nothing now there will be time for women's time

International Women's Gulf Peace Initiative

Margarita Papandreou

I write as a feminist peace activist. Feminism is important to me. It is an ideological and political framework by which I can judge events and developments around me and in the world. It provides me with both tools for analysis and coping skills. It is very useful in my everyday life. Feminism for me goes beyond the issue of gender differences and human rights; it has made me sensitive to manipulation and the use of power to exploit groups or persons in the context of economic and power disparities.

In a sense, feminism is the eyeglasses I have put on my brain to see with clarity what is really being done by those who have the

---

Editor's Note—Margarita Papandreou is president of the Center for Research and Action on Peace (Greece) and is the Global Network Coordinator for Women for Mutual Security (international).

As the former First Lady of Greece, she helped found the Women's Union of Greece, a nationwide, independent feminist organization in 1976. She was influential in pressing for numerous reforms enhancing the legal and social status of women in Greek society, abolishing the dowry system, introducing civil marriage, legalizing abortion, and securing pensions for farm women. The network she has created has been represented at every US–USSR Summit, as well as at NATO and Warsaw Pact meetings. She is the author of *Nightmares in Athens*, which documents the Greek military dictatorship.

power to deceive—by CNN, for example, when it reports on the Persian Gulf War—or to understand the methods and techniques of the rhetoric of the Bush administration. It enables me to read the *Herald Tribune* or any other newspaper and to deal with the distortion and lies being fed to the public. It helps me recognize the reasons why Palestinian women are totally ignored in the American press, or why their nationalism is described only in anti-Zionist terms, or why their role in the Palestinian cause is portrayed as male-manipulated political mouthpieces.

These eyeglasses help me to understand when there is an effort to confuse me, to make me feel helpless, to take away my voice of protest. Feminism gives me the strength not to fall into that trap, to know that I cannot curl up in my personal shell and allow others to proceed with their nefarious work. It gives me courage to speak and write and give my account of the lessons of the Gulf War, its impact on women, and the challenges that we face in the days ahead.

As a feminist, I reject the simplistic statement that "men make war, women make peace" because I think it is more true to say that those in power make war while those out of power make peace. Having said that, I believe that in the case of the Persian Gulf War we did have an instance of masculinity gone berserk. On one hand, you had an American president who felt emasculated by being called a "wimp" and who was determined to wipe out that image once and for all. You also had an America which felt emasculated by the so-called "Vietnam Syndrome." Bush's upbeat, hormonal taking command stance, his ultimatum-type pronouncements, and refusal at every turn to take any steps in the direction of dialogue or negotiation—all of which he saw as "sissy," "soft," "appeasing," and undoubtedly too feminine an approach—allowed us to witness, reel after reel, a live Rambo show, the honest-to-god gutsy man of the twenty-first century.

On the other hand was Saddam Hussein, a man whose ego, whose personal ambition, whose sense that any concession, any flexibility in his position would be a sign of weakness and would humiliate him in the Arab world. Again, all these are strong masculine traits and contributed to this testosterone game which made two male personalities a critical factor in the inevitability of the war. The key responsibility lies, however, with the macho Bush who consistently refused to discuss at all any number of proposals from Iraq and other nations for a peaceful resolution [For the record, proposals for a negotiated settlement which included Iraqi withdrawal from Kuwait were offered on August 12 and 19, October 18, December 20, January 15, and February 22. Bush refused to consider any of them often charging that any settlement short of a humiliating military defeat would allow Saddam to "save face" among Arab people — *editor*]. He seemed almost psychopathically fixated on a massive, bloody, destructive, and punitive war—provided all the suffering was on the other side.

I want to turn now to the account of our first journey to Baghdad in the last days of peace before the U.S.-led bombers began the destruction of Iraq and the killing of its people. We were an international brigade of women taking a big step and a big risk for the cause of peace. It all started on the afternoon of Sunday, January 7, 1991 in Athens. Flora from Moscow was at the Iraqi Embassy getting her visa, Joan and Kay from the U.S. were at the Jordanian Embassy doing the same. I was collecting last minute items, trying to remember what I wanted to take to the Federation of Iraqi Women: newspaper articles, a letter from "Peace by Candlelight," peace messages, chocolates, peace bird pins. Maude from Canada was sitting in my living room leafing through news reports on the Persian Gulf crisis. The mood was one of urgency and desperation.

In haste, we began calling ourselves the International Women's Gulf Peace Initiative. Our journey would take us through Cairo, Egypt, to pick up Nawal al-Saadawl of the Arab Women's Solidarity Association, and in Amman, Jordan, Fathieh, representing the same organization. With seven women from various corners of the earth, we went with one dream and one hope—that we could work out a peace plan with Iraqi Women that might be acceptable to the male leadership of both nations.

Despite this noble dream, we were not naive. Peace actions never have a guarantee of success. One does them first of all out of faith— the faith that if enough people engage in such actions, the world would be different. And second, we are beginning to discover that doing something takes away the terrible sense of helplessness women have as the Big Boys play the game and make all the decisions.

From Amman we headed by plane for foggy Baghdad, only to be directed to another airport in Basrah, the southern most Iraqi town on the Persian Gulf next to Kuwait, and the town which was being described as the future "front line." Women and children were taken to the Sheraton for the night, and I found myself happy for discrimination. Men slept on the hard benches of the airport.

When I came down to the lobby in the morning, the beautiful, shining faces of three young women greeted me from behind the reception counter. Their faces were skillfully made-up, the coloring in harmony with the sweaters and scarves they were wearing. False nails in bright red finished off the picture of modern woman. Here was the *femme fatale*, the unveiled woman, whose all-absorbing and destructive power according to the Muslim interpretation makes men lose their self-control. According to what I have read, they must be controlled to prevent men from being distracted from their religious and social responsibilities.

"O, god," I thought. "Let them use that power to distract men from war! Let them be the Arab Lysystrates! Could we reach out over cultural differences or over political differences with Iraqi women and build a common front?"

"Good-morning," they said with just a touch of an accent. My stomach twitched. Would bombs change their relaxed warmth to terror and fear? Was an ugly war going to destroy their vibrancy, their freshness, their future? The stark contrast between these warm faces and the impending horror of war haunts me still.

Finally, we caught another plane to Baghdad. We were impressed immediately with the outward appearance of normalcy. The women who met us at the airport came with flowers. It was agreed that we would start our discussions at 5 p.m. and stay as late as we needed the first day to cover the issues.

Manal Younis, the president of the Federation of Iraqi Women was not present at the meeting because she was on the Peace Ship impounded in the port of Omkasr. She and several hundred women peace activists, also from various parts of the world, were unable to get

Top — Alamara, Iraq: members of the Federation of Iraqi Women pose with delegates of the Women's Gulf Peace Initiative in front of a bombed out house.
Bottom — Another destroyed neighborhood in Alamara, apparently from B-52 carpet bombing. No military installations are anywhere near. In spite of U.S. government claims, the bombing did massively destroy civilian property. Less than 7% of the total bomb tonnage dropped was the laser guided type. The continued embargo will make rebuilding Iraq nearly impossible.

through the Gulf blockade to bring their cargo of medicines, milk and other food products to Iraq. I worried that her absence might affect the likelihood of our seeing Saddam Hussein. She was a loyal and trusted aide to the President, with considerable influence. As head of an organization of several million women, she had played a key role in mobilizing them in the Iran-Iraq war and was now doing the same in preparation for another. On the other hand, I felt relieved. Her militancy and commitment to Hussein might have been an obstacle to a softer approach to the situation, to what we were hoping to do in our discussions—woman-to-woman.

Our talks started in the elegant quarters of the executive office of the organization. The Federation owns a huge three-story building with assembly halls, committee rooms, areas for craft displays, and lounges. I thought with some dismay of the tiny quarters we had for Women for Mutual Security in downtown Athens. But, then, the Federation is a government organization.

Looming over us was the presence of Saddam Hussein. Huge photographs graced the walls, the smaller framed pictures sat on all the flat surfaces; there he was with his family, with workers, with children, and with many members of the Federation down through the years.

After a round of introductions, the Iraqi women brought up the Peace Ship and described the mistreatment of the women by the navy men who boarded the boat as part of the economic blockade. Apparently there were goods on board which the soldiers felt violated the U.N. imposed sanctions, and the boat had been forced to dock at Omkasr. We sent the women a message of solidarity.

Women from the Federation spoke first. It was a litany which we were to hear many times in the course of our conversations with them and with the officials of the government. What happened in Kuwait was not an invasion. Kuwait belongs to Iraq. Its borders were drawn by occupying colonial powers in an arbitrary manner, in their own imperialist power interests. The situation in Kuwait was being used by America and Israel who were frightened by the strength of Iraq after its war with Iran and now wanted to provoke another war to reduce the strength of Iraq.

"Now, after eight years of war and only two years of peace, we must defend Iraq from foreign invasion." Aza was saying this. She was a woman of about fifty, conservatively dressed and very thin.

"Do you want war?" Maude asked.

In one voice, the six Iraqi women from the Executive Board replied, "No!" Each one started telling about her losses in the Iran-Iraq war. There was a deep melancholy in their souls which came to the surface as they spoke of the loved ones killed or missing.

"Then can we talk about a way to avoid war?" Flora suggested. The answer was in the affirmative.

We outlined our plan. The first step must be a withdrawal of all foreign troops from the Gulf area. They shook their heads in agreement. But it turned out that foreign troops to them meant the so-called multi-national forces, the U.S. and allied countries whose troops were now massively staged in Saudia Arabia and other Gulf Nations. We meant those armies, but we also meant the Iraqi forces in Kuwait.

This was the true point of contention. Whatever else was said about our plan for peace was perfectly acceptable to them. The interesting aspect of our debate on the status of Kuwait—and which was true subsequently in our discussions with government officials—was that although the position seemed intransigent, little slivers of flexibility always crept in, sometimes by a longer silence in response to a question and sometimes through the use of certain words for framing of the issue. One minister told us clearly that "we could contemplate that [a withdrawal]" and then ended up by reiterating that Kuwait belongs to Iraq.

We built strong friendships with the women we met during the three days we were there. This in spite of or maybe because of the evil spectre of war which hung over all our conversations. The Iraqi women looked to us for some assurance that it wouldn't happen, or that maybe we had the power to affect the course of world events. We also had a feeling that they relied on the figure that dominated their offices—Saddam Hussein—to find a way to keep them out of a new war.

In the end, we came out with a common statement for our press conference, one that was largely a statement of principles and an appeal for peace. In the interest of fairness, they were willing to remove language that was sharply critical of the position taken by the United States. But they could not sign a peace plan that designated a withdrawal from Kuwait. However, they agreed that the International Women's Gulf Peace Initiative could present its own view at the press conference and that they would be present to introduce us and somehow to give silent approval.

We wanted to stop a war. They did too. We had the freedom to say it. They had only the freedom to desire it. As women we touched base. As citizens living in different systems we struck out.

Having recounted all this, a short description by a concerned Western observer, I must add that when I react to my stay in Baghdad with my gut, when I release my feelings and emotions from my own cultural bias, I respond differently. *When I become one of them*, I experience the sense of oppression, the suffocation of years of colonial rule, the humiliation of being seen as an Arab stereotype—helpless, ineffective, unworthy. And then I begin to think differently.

They concluded their statement with what can only be taken as a testimony to their courage and strength: "And I say, we don't want war. But if it comes, we will face it with courage and determination, and even if we lose in fact we will emerge with our pride and dignity intact. We will not be humbled anymore by foreign intervention. Our spirit will never be broken."

Our failed peace initiative enables me to make at least one point in retrospect: that while we women have many things in common as women—and certainly our second class citizenship and oppression are key among them—there are also obstacles to our unity, obstacles which we must try to overcome, or if not overcome, to understand. There are religious differences, political differences, ethnic differences. These are the blinders. These are the restrictions. And these same things may sometimes serve as our security.

What I gained from the trip was an ability to understand ultimately and emotionally how I would feel in their place. Intellectually, I understand that these women were obliged to stick by the party line, that the obstacle to a full and free debate—as women—was mostly political or party discipline. They were not in a position to present a women's peace platform to their party elders. I recognize, of course, that party discipline is important in the struggle against imperialism. Also, women are not yet supposed to deal with issues of war and peace. That, by the way, is not so different from most of our western countries.

My point in this writing is, however, not to argue for understanding cultural differences. Such differences between the Arab World and the West do indeed exist, but I want particularly to consider how these differences are distorted, how they are twisted, as a political tool to form public opinion in favor of a war, an intervention, and an occupation.

On one hand, there has been a long campaign to persuade the people in the West of the inferiority of the Arab people; and on the other, a dearth of information about something so simple as the history of the Middle East. And one needn't have to make a long a deep study. Just state the fact that the borders of the regions were imposed by Western colonialists—British, French, American—intent on controlling oil and monopolizing trade with the Far East. Western powers have always also been intent on insuring that no one strong Arab nation would emerge to challenge the imperial powers. That fact alone gives one insight into the whole picture. These are the things we must know in order to neutralize the poison—"the selling of the Gulf War"—with whatever means we have as a movement.

Since we are women and since I have made two trips to Baghdad now to work with the Federation of Iraqi Women—the first to work out a woman's peace plan that could be acceptable to both sides and the second to collect facts on the effects of the war on women and children to determine their needs and to talk about their role in the future—I want to tell you the way in which propaganda is used about the Muslim woman in order to manipulate Western thinking and to create a general reaction to her "low status" among people who couldn't care less about the question of equality between the sexes.

It is a well-established habit to compare the Muslin woman to the Western woman. Questions about the liberation of the Muslim woman, about her oppression by the religious system she lives under

Rick Reinhard / IMPACT VISUALS
Ruins of Iraqi telecommunications center in Baghdad. This building lies between an old Armenian Church and a major business area—both of which were heavily damaged. On June 22, 1991, U.S. officials finally admitted what had been obvious to many observers all along: "Some targets, especially late in the war, were bombed primarliy to create postwar leverage over Iraq, not to influence the course of the conflict itself . . . the intent was to destroy or damage valuable facilities that Baghdad could not repair without foreign assistance" (*Washington Post*, June 23, 1991: A1).

and about which culture makes the woman more of a second-class citizen have blocked a true analysis of the Muslim woman's real situation. Muslim men are described as promiscuous and women as having to endure a terrible fate.

I read once a wonderful statement by an Arab woman. She said, "Harem, the veil, polygamy are synonymous in the West with female oppression. Whether the harem can justifiably be defined as exclusively a device for oppressing women I won't get into now. As for polygamy and the veil, it would be quite easy to argue that neither is by definition more oppressive than monogamy and no veil."

In this constant barrage of propaganda and attack, Muslim women often found themselves out of self-defense defending anachronistic traditions which they themselves had begun to deplore. The fact that Western colonizers and some Western feminists took on the responsibility of painting Muslim women as un-liberated, mistreated, unhappy pawns in the hands of men made any campaign for changes in her condition, in case she so desired, appear to be a case of succumbing to foreign influences. We all remember the women during the Iranian revolution who put their veils back on in defiance of Western values and Western imperialism.

I don't think it is worth talking about how women are treated in the Muslim East or the Christian West. Sexual inequality exists in both systems. But it is when these biases are used to elicit reactions that are negative, that they become part of a defamation plan to justify actions against the Arab world. Then we have to understand how important it is to fight the technique of stereotyping. Once in the States, an American woman said to me that they had numerous sources—all of them, of course, Western—that women, according to Islam, had no soul and were thought of simply as animals.

When I returned to Baghdad for my second visit, I sought out the same women of the Federation I had seen before the war. More of them were in black. Before the war there had been a tension, certainly, but a hope, a belief, and an illusion that there would be no war. I left Baghdad on the first trip convinced that there would be a war but buoyed up by their convictions. This time there was melancholy and depression, but more than that a bitterness, cynicism,

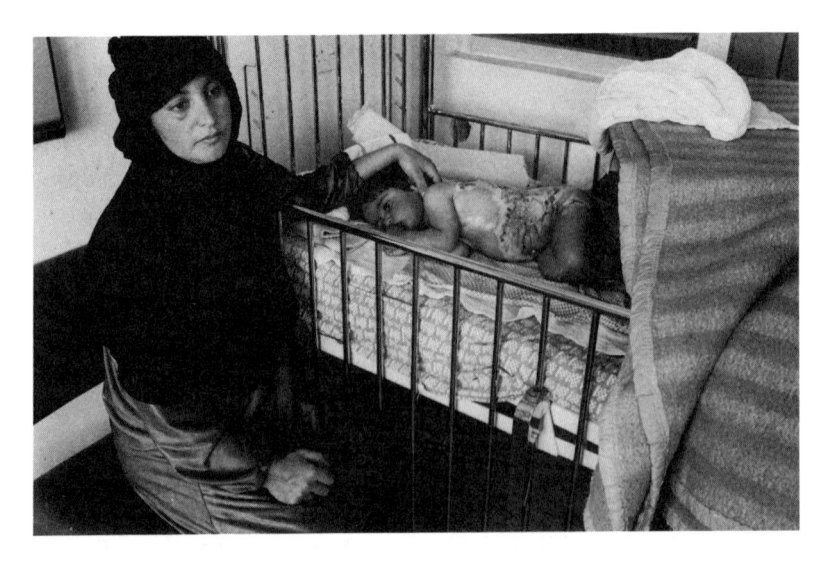

Rick Reinhard / IMPACT VISUALS

In the Baghdad Children's Hospital, a mother comforts her badly burned 2-year old daughter. Bush's new war strategy avoids direct military killing but rather destroys the civilian support infrastructure such as water, food, fuel, hospital and medical supplies, and sanitation industries and then permits the population to die from disease, malnutrition and exposure. Of course, women and children suffer first and most.

---

and a fatalism. They didn't believe that anyone of good intentions could do anything. They were convinced that the forces merging to create the war were long in preparation, and opposition forces—whatever or wherever they were—had been whistling in the dark to attempt to overturn already fated events. They expressed no doubt about the decisions of their government. They were not bowed. They had not conceded defeat, but they were emotionally exhausted.

The victims of the war were the women and children—the classic victims. They are suffering from the kind of war this was—a sort of policy of "bomb now and the dying will come later." By the time of our visit in mid-May the number of people killed from direct bomb hits had been far exceeded by those who have died from the damage to the infrastructure of the country and the insurrections which occurred in fifteen of eighteen regions of Iraq. We spent several days seeing both types of destruction. We were affected by the physical and material destruction. But we were much more affected by the faces of babies and young children who were sick and dying from dehydration, malnutrition, and water-bourn diseases. For babies born during the period of the war, their mother's state of shock stopped the production of breast milk. And in many cases there was no substitute. Dysentery as a result of contaminated water and food is rampant—all of this from the destruction of water and sewage systems and electrical plants needed to work purification systems and to keep foods refrigerated. The expectation is that now that summer is coming the cases of diseases like typhoid or cholera will rise dramatically. A doctor in the hospital in Alamara told us his story. He was speaking to an American and told him of the need of a particular medicine. "But you would need tons of that. We can't send you that," the American replied. "But you sent us tons of bombs," was the doctor's reply.

Within the women and among the people is a wellspring of rage. This is just the latest chapter of colonial interference. While Arabs are still dying, especially the little ones, and the embargo on food, medicine, industrial equipment such as water purification equipment continue, Americans stage huge victory celebrations in their land of plenty and gloat in explicit satisfaction that their own lives are all that is important. The blare of brass bands and the glare yellow ribbons deafen and blind them to the suffering they have caused for others, whose lives they consider of little importance.

The economic benefits of this war will accrue to certain classes and strata. The rich will get richer; the poor will get poorer and the poorest of the poor—women—will suffer even more.

Statement Made to the Press — Baghdad, May 21 1991

We represent a group of women who are spokespeople for international women's peace networks, and who are connected to the

the group which came here prior to the war on an International Women's Gulf Peace Initiative.

We failed in our first mission—to have any impact on the forces that be—to affect events in anyway to stop this ugly war. Now we are here to assess the effect of that war on women and children particularly, but on the population more generally. We want to determine the urgent immediate needs, for humanitarian action, and because we are peace activists, the political steps that the Peace movement can engage in to bring some semblance of normality to this region. We want to try to understand all the factors that went into the making of this war and to determine where the peace movement might have acted to more effectively deter the war. In other words, what can non-governmental organizations do—if anything—to achieve social justice, economic justice, and peace in the world.

We come in solidarity with the Iraqi people and not in support of any particular political ideology or leadership. In fact as women, we are suspicious of all leadership, partly because it is male, and men have been trained in all our societies to be aggressive and to take control, and partly because we see how power corrupts and becomes an aim in itself, denying the human factor. As individuals we have no personal stake in the mission we have set up for ourselves; we are not running for political office, we can neither gain nor lose by our activities. We are searching for the truth, and something that has motivated us initially has been the clever suppression of the facts about Iraq, and the Middle East in general, and the distortion of the information when it was given.

Those of us who live in the Western world have had to work hard to understand the cultural milieu of the Arab world and overcome the dangerous ignorance that the West has displayed about the cultural, historical, political, and social dimensions which are part of the collective memory and aspirations of this region of the world.

We begin by saying that none of us here have accepted the invasion of Kuwait. We understand the arguments of the Iraqis—that Kuwait was created in the desert in 1922 by a British diplomat drawing a red line on a map; that there were nine little sheikdoms that suddenly appeared in this oil producing area of the Middle East; that Kuwait was historically a county in the nation of Iraq;, and that Iraq was the only country not to vote for its admission to the United Nations. These sheikdoms are drenched in money, oil, and gold with a total population of half a million people surrounded by a sea of poor people. And when Kuwait took actions affecting the economic life of Iraq—killing the country—Saddam was right to be angry and furious. He was not right, however, to take Kuwait over by force.

Having said that, however, the U.S. was not right to have moved to reverse the situation by the use of force. It was not the first time that an Arab country aggressed against another in modern times: Libya's incursion into Tunisia, Morocco's invasion of the Sahara, Egypt's incursions into Yemen, Algeria's into Morocco, etc. And other non-Arab incursions in the Middle East include Israel's invasion and annexation of the West Bank, Gaza Strip, and Golan Heights; Turkey's occupation of Cyprus. All of these invasions and occupations have been condemned by the United Nations and yet none of these resolutions have been implemented as yet, let alone by force.

These are not facts we learned here in our discussions. But they are necessarily part of our analysis and part of our investigation.

What we did learn here is that those who have suffered most from this war and are still suffering are the women and children—the classic victims. They are suffering from the kind of war this was—a sort of policy of "bomb now and the dying will come later." By now the number of people dead from direct bomb hits is far less than those who have died from the damage to the infrastructure of this country and the subsequent rebellions in fifteen regions of Iraq. These days we have visited several areas to see both types of destruction, but we were much more affected by the faces of babies and young children who were sick and dying from malnutrition and dehydration. For babies born during the period of the war, their mother's state of shock stopped the manufacture of breast milk. In many cases there was no substitute. Dysentery as a result of contaminated water and food is rampant—all this from the destruction of water and sewage systems and electrical plants needed to run water and sewage treatment facilities. The expectation is that now that summer is coming, the cases of diseases will rise dramatically. A doctor in the hospital in Alamara told us this story: he was speaking to an American and telling him of the need for a particular medicine. "But you would need tons of that, we can't send you that," the American replied. "But you sent us tons of bombs," was the reply.

So medical supplies and foodstuffs are of urgent need.

We also feel that all economic sanctions should be withdrawn. Iraq complied with all UN requests and resolutions. It has been damaged extensively. Holding on to sanctions now for some additional political purpose is cruel and unusual punishment. And the leadership does not suffer. The babies, mothers, and fathers do suffer.

The driving concern of U.S. policy—that is, to make certain no indigenous power gains substantial control over the oil reserves of the region—has been satisfied. Now is the time to allow the people of Iraq to reconstruct their country. We hope that reconstruction will include a reconstruction of the system toward more individual freedoms, democratic participation, and multi-parties. We have reason to believe from our discussions that this is the intended direction.

We will continue to push for an International Peace Conference on the Middle East to deal with the Arab-Israeli conflict and a resolution of the Palestinian issue, although we are not confident that the conditions created by this war are conducive to any success.

We will work for stopping the arms race and for the disarmament of the Middle East, including nuclear disarmament. This is not just a regional goal for us but a world goal.

We will be working for better international bodies, and for reform of the U.N. to make it more democratic and more representative of the peoples of the world and not the power establishments of the world.

We conclude by saying that we stand by the principle of non-violent resolution to the problems of conflict.

International Women's Gulf Peace Initiative

Dictatorship In Fiji

Kuini Bavadra

In accepting the leadership of the Fiji Labour Party and its coalition with the National Federation Party after the death of my husband and former Party Leader and Prime Minister, I was and still am very mindful of how he perceived such a role. Above all, the call of leadership was one of selfless service to the people. He believed that whether it was hereditary or elective, leadership necessarily entailed responsibility for the common good, not an entitlement to personal prerogatives. His belief was in harmony with our traditional concept of leadership.

Editor's Note — The people of Fiji pioneered the nuclear-free South Pacific movement, demanding an end to port calls by all ships that were nuclear powered or that carried nuclear weapons. The government of the United States saw this positions as a threat to their control of the Pacific.

Dr. Timoci Uluivuda Bavadra was a strong supporter of the nuclear-free movement as well as an appointed head of the coalition of the Fijian Labour Party and National Federation Party (NFP). On April 12, 1987, he was sworn in as Prime Minister of Fiji. One month later on May 14, 1987, a military coup led by Major General Sitiveni Robuka deposed Prime Minister Bavadra, incarcerating him and all the members of his government.

Simione Durutalo, former Vice-President of the Fiji Labour Party, stated that Ratu Sir Kamisese Mara and others in the Alliance Party were merely pawns and not the real force behind the coup (Lal, V. 1990). Noor Dean, Deputy Speaker of the now-deposed Bavadra government, said he was positive that the so-called Fijian soldiers who invaded his parliament were in fact U.S. Marines.

This paper written by Adi Kuini Vuekaba Bavadra, Timoci Bavadra's widow and successor to the leadership of the NFP-Labour coalition describes the effect which the coup has had upon her country.

It was a leadership code that Timoci personally lived by. It meant a number of things: not living a life that was detached from the people and their concerns, but being among them and helping them to understand the issues involved in the current political crisis in Fiji. He believed in shared decision-making and consultation rather than an authoritarian style of management. Above all, a distinctive feature of Timoci's leadership was his personal humility and modesty. These qualities enabled him to inspire loyalty in those who worked with him.

The Coalition came to power in 1987 on the strength of a com prehensive program of social reform intended to improve the living standards of ordinary working people irrespective of their race or creed. To this end, and after just a month of office, the Coalition government introduced a number of reforms such as the abolition of hospital outpatient fees and free public transport for the old and needy. Since the coup, the drastic deterioration in living standards and the rising costs of essential goods and services has made the widening gap between the rich and poor even more visible and has made the need for social reform all the more urgent.

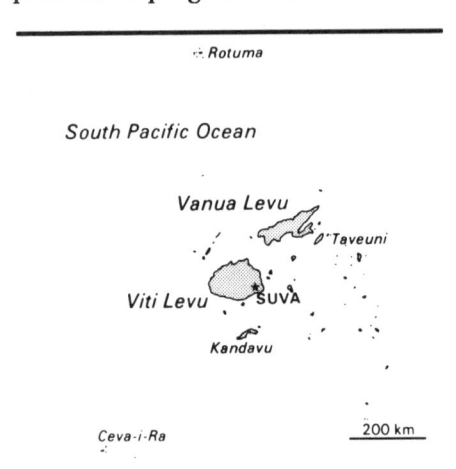

Fiji
Independent from United Kingdom since 1970. Government control by military coup since 1987. Population, 759,567: 49% Indian, 46% Fijian, 5% European. Total area, 18,270 km².

Meanwhile, the post-coup administration continues to display a cavalier attitude to the plight of the poor and the under privileged whose numbers are steadily rising. Economic recovery since the military coup is evident from the regained buoyancy of certain industries and a 12.5% growth rate in 1989 for instance. Those of us who live with ordinary working class people in urban areas, as well as in villages and rural settlements, cannot help but notice with deep concern, however, that the "trumpeting" of this economic achievement at the *macro* level has not been borne out by *visible* or "tangible signs" for the people. The Coalition's policies for material advancement today remain shaped by the human values of social justice and equality. These values will ultimately determine the quality of life for ourselves and our children rather than the country's economic growth or foreign reserves. As a party, we recognize that people are our country's most precious resource. We, therefore, insist that access to decent housing and health care, free education, meaningful employment, and just wages should be a fundamental right of everyone, not the prerogative of the few. A fairer distribution of wealth remains our central goal so that the benefits of developing our rich land, sea, and mineral resources do not continue to be monopolized by a powerful minority.

Another stated principle of the Coalition as it entered the 1987 elections was that no government of Fiji should represent the interests of one race or religion. At the time, the drastic events that followed so closely on the heels of the party's victory could not have been foreseen. The ugly racism and religious bigotry orchestrated to create fear, suspicion, and disunity have left deep scars on our people. Worse still, such shameful values appear to have won official endorsement.

Since the illegal overthrow of the Coalition government along with the 1970 Independence Constitution, my party has consistently called on the military-installed interim administration for dialogue with us as representatives of the people who still hold the official and legal mandate of the people of Fiji. It is our firm opinion that only through involving the Coalition party in the negotiations for a fair constitution, can there be some hope for a restoration of a mutual sense of trust and respect between the various ethnic communities in Fiji.

Our calls for dialogue and consultation have up to today, however, been totally ignored by the interim administration which has made up its mind to pursue a disastrous course according to its own will and in a moot, arrogant, undemocratic, and dictatorial manner.

The culmination of this extreme sense of arrogance has been the imposition by decree in July 1990 of a Constitution which has received widespread condemnation from fair-minded people within

Fiji, as well as in Australia, New Zealand, Britain, and the United States. The most repugnant feature of this so-called Constitution is the primacy it gives to ethnic Fijians at the expense of other ethnic groups. The unequal representation and the reservation of certain senior public service posts for Fijians contradict the basic principles of democracy and justice that have come to be cherished by our citizens. Even worse, this Constitution threatens to sow the seeds of dissension, violence, and destruction.

Moreover, such a discriminatory measure will never resolve the problems that face the majority of my Fijian brothers and sisters. Nor can they ever be justified on the basis of affirmative action. The principle of affirmative action is to restore balance in situations of social inequality and disadvantage, never to create a Master Race. Yet, racial supremacy lies at the heart of the Constitution. And it is compounded by the retrograde proposal to introduce a wholly communal system of representation which will only encourage communal divisions and strife.

In its present form, this so-called Constitution will not even benefit the Fijian people as a whole. The imbalance in regional representation and the denial of fair representation for urban Fijians, for instance, will cause bitterness, disaffection, and greater national disunity. Similarly, the vesting of unchallengeable powers in a non-elected body of high chiefs removes accountability from the people. The principle of accountability is not only crucial to parliamentary democracy, but it is also in keeping with the spirit of traditional Fijian leadership. We in the Coalition still insist up to today that as the supreme law of the land the new Constitution should be a democratic and just one, acceptable to the majority of our people. Since being illegally and unceremoniously thrown out of government, we have consistently called on the governments in the South Pacific, as well as democratic governments in the Commonwealth to try and convince the interim administration of Fiji that it has a moral obligation to broaden the process of constitution-making by allowing for open dialogue and the fullest consultation with the chosen representatives of the people.

Because the Indian government made a lot of noise in criticizing the interim administration's single-minded approach in not consulting

Dictatorship in Fiji — *41*

with the people on this undemocratic and racist Constitution, I was not entirely surprised when I was on an official tour in Australia last June to be summoned to attend to an urgent telephone inquiry by a journalist about the expulsion order given to the Indian Embassy. Yes, the Indian Embassy was told to pack up and leave—this affected about fifty staff members of the Embassy and their families. By that action, Fiji's interim administration was determined to tell the international community that it was not going to tolerate any form of criticism from any of them, irrespective of how well-founded or how morally sound the criticism levelled at the post-coup administration was.

Last year also saw the expulsions of two regional Fiji-based media organizations—PACNEWS and PACBROAD—organizations which were responsible for training indigenous Pacific print and radio journalists. Apparently, these media organizations had become too professional and effective in acting as clearing houses for news on Fiji politics. The irony of this particular expulsion is that the Pacific journalists who became victims of the situation also included journalists working for the Fiji's Ministry of Information. Information Minister Kobuabola has become a household name in the Pacific as well as for overseas journalists as a result of his intolerant and arrogant attitude to media personnel in general.

As recent as November of 1990, an unprecedented announcement was also made in Fiji that Australia's Minister for Foreign Affairs, Senator Gareth Evans, was not welcome to visit Fiji as part of his scheduled tour of the South Pacific. Senator Evans has apparently been victimized as a result of a speech he delivered in the General Assembly of the U.N. in New York where, among other issues he raised, was a paragraph or two on the unsatisfactory political development in Fiji. Senator Evans also criticized the racist and undemocratic nature of the new Constitution in post-coup Fiji. This principled pronouncement by Senator Evans has made him unpopular in the eyes of Fiji's interim administration—a newspaper item explaining why the Minister's planned visit to Fiji was not welcomed said Senator Evans had apparently "swallowed the Coalition line"— hence his criticism of post-coup Fiji and the Constitution at the U.N.

In response to an inquiry by a local journalist, I made the following remarks: "Senator Evans has not swallowed the Coalition line, but only swallowed the truth and had the moral courage to take a principled stand." Such is the intolerant attitude of Fiji's interim administration towards any objective criticism levelled at them.

Looking at the response of the U.N. to the action taken by Saddam Hussein in the invasion of Kuwait has made me cynical, however, about the role of the U.N. and to what extent it is controlled by the superpowers in order that other member nations would always dance to their tune. I'm quite certain that if Fiji were as richly endowed with oil which could have an undermining effect on the economic interests of the leading superpowers, the U.N. could have by now taken a concerted effort in condemning the invasion of basic human rights in my country through the illegal overthrow of the democratically-elected government and the political developments thereafter.

You see, what we have in place in Fiji since the 1987 military coup is an unelected government which is determined to rule according to the whims of one or two individuals. It is not accountable to anyone for its actions and is free to use millions of dollars of taxpayers' money and aid money according to its own terms. Those people who dance to the interim government's tune are singled out for promotions in the Public Service; their children are given top priority for scholarships. The regions which are politically favored are given high priority in the allocation of development funds and so on and so forth.

This is a severe invasion of our peoples' basic human rights. Every human being should be given the right to live in a society free of oppression and discrimination. Every decent country should protest loudly when the people of another country are deprived of their basic human rights because of the color of their skin or because they happen to support one political party against another.

One of my favorite Gandhi quotes goes like this: "When the law is pernicious, we should respond to a higher moral order." Friends, in Fiji today, the law that ordinary people are now compelled to live by is grossly and blatantly pernicious. I appeal to you, therefore, to respond to a higher moral order by lobbying on our behalf with your organizations and your governments.

United States Military Bases And Their Impact On Women In The Philippines

Petite O. Peredo

It is now a matter of months before the 1947 Military Bases Agreement (MBA) between the United States and the Republic of the Philippines is scheduled to expire on September 16, 1991. That is, of course, if the current Philippine government chooses to heed the already widespread anti-base sentiment in the country today and —this once—genuinely protect Philippine national interests prior to

---

Editor's Note—In 1988 Petite Peredo became National Secretary-General of GABRIELA (General Assembly Binding Women for Reform, Integrity, Equality, Leadership, and Action), a coalition of one hundred and one women's groups. The coalition was named for a brave woman in Philippine colonial history who led a people's movement against the Spanish colonizers. The overwhelming portion of their membership comes from the grass-roots—peasant women, workers and urban poor. Their struggle centers on women's rights and the Filipino people's movement for sovereignty, democracy, peace, and justice.

The status of women in the Philippines is the legacy of an earlier feudal structure that underlies the economy and culture. The presence of the U.S. military further degrades the Filipino woman by using her as a commodity and object of pleasure. The constant economic crisis faced by the Filipinos has forced many women into prostitution and has created the market known as "mail order brides." GABRIELA has laid the groundwork against sexism and in support of the rights of women to participate in shaping the future of the Philippines.

Sadly, however, President Corazon Aquino and her government (led by Foreign Affairs Secretary Raul Manglapus) are obviously otherwise inclined. Developments in recent months strongly indicate a pro-bases position in the government, in spite of a few dissenting voices in the Senate and Congress. The Philippine stance in this year's September exploratory talks is in fact already a virtual declaration of the Aquino administration's intention to allow the extension of U.S. military presence in Philippine territory. This early, discussions in government and pro-administration quarters are already veering towards the terms of a possible new bases treaty with the United States even as bases conversion studies in the legislature are still underway.

Meanwhile, on the American side, it has always been evident that the U.S. government will not easily relinquish its military stronghold in the Asia-Pacific region. It is in fact ready to topple the current Philippine government through covert political intervention (by supporting a right-wing *coup d'état*) or direct armed aggression should the current government decide to endanger the continuing existence of U.S. bases in this country. Neither will it stop short of eliminating Filipino nationalists fighting for the proposal to immediately dismantle and thereafter completely reject all foreign military bases in this land. Proof of the U.S. design is in the formulation and implementation by American militarists of the notorious Low Intensity Conflict doctrine that has already claimed the lives of hundreds of Filipino anti-base activists.

There simply could be no truth to the erstwhile pronouncements of U.S. officials that they are willing to dismantle their bases here if they are so required and are even now already scouting for alternative sites where they could set up their military installations. We in the Philippines are aware that the shaky condition of the American economy could not at this point foot a $12 billion bill for the transfer of the United States' largest military bases overseas. Current strains on the U.S. military budget likewise runs counter to expected increases in the maintenance costs of these bases in a new location. It must be noted that the meager amounts doled out to the Philippines as economic and military aid, also now considered as base rentals, are at a minimum when compared to U.S. expenditures in the maintenance of any other American military base elsewhere in the world. In the final analysis, the United States is more likely to intervene in local political power struggles if only to ensure the installation of a regime that favors the U.S. bases and its other interests in the Philippines.

Apart from these financial considerations I have mentioned, the determination of the United States to keep its bases in the Philippines at all costs primarily stems from the very strategic location of our country. Clark Air Base in Pampanga, Subic Naval Base in Zambales and the twenty other smaller installations currently operating here are within easy striking distance of the rest of Southeast Asia, Mainland China, Indonesia, Korea, the Middle East, Australia and the islands of the Pacific. They comprise the primary line of U.S. defense in the Pacific Ocean and serve as the main springboard for American intervention and imperialism in the whole Asia-Pacific region. They have, therefore, assumed a very vital role in the global projection of U.S. military supremacy and the preservation of American economic hegemony in the Asian-Pacific region.

These past two months, the strategic value of these bases has again been underlined with the eruption of the Iraq-Kuwait conflict. Intent on preserving its stronghold in the Persian Gulf, the United States has once again taken an active combative role in the Middle East problem. During the war, Clark and Subic were revved up to full battle gear to serve as the main base from which to launch American war operations, where combat supplies will be stored and damaged war equipment will be repaired. Naturally, they will also serve the needs of servicemen stopping for recuperation, rest, and recreation. These developments, we expect, will of course further strengthen the resolve of American policy makers pushing for the continued upkeep of their bases in the Philippines. U.S. Assistant Secretary of Defense Carl Ford said, "The facilities at Clark and Subic were extremely important to our Persian Gulf War effort—tremendous amounts of materiel passed through the bases annd some forces transited the Philippines enroute to the Gulf (qtd. in *Pacific News Bulletin*, June 1991: p. 8).

Likewise a clear indication of the United States' adamant refusal to leave the Philippines is the barrage of indirect and direct pro-base propaganda they have released to the public. Through the United States Information Agency (USIA), reading and visual materials on the desirability of the military bases for Filipinos are pouring into the tri-media and educational institutions, particularly in the countrysides. At the same time, disinformation and smear campaigns discrediting people's organizations, especially those openly espousing an anti-bases position, continue. The traditional red-scare campaign and various forms of harassment are targeted at anti-bases groups and there are enough reasons to suspect American covert involvement in these undertakings.

In view of all the things that I have mentioned, it has become paramount for us in non-government organizations to take up the issue of the U.S. bases and their ill effects on the Filipino people as a primary concern in our operations and campaigns. Likewise, we continually seek to inform our people that *there are* viable and economically lucrative alternatives to the maintenance of those bases in our country. We believe that it is the people's right to know what possible options exist other than those espoused by the incumbent government which has consistently proven itself subservient to American interests and dictates in the first place.

Ours is certainly a long and difficult struggle, especially now that the country is increasingly being militarized even as the President continues to claim her government's adherence to free expression and democratic processes. Dispersals of our peaceful public assemblies are becoming more and more violent. Hundreds from our ranks have been wounded. Many have been arrested and incarcerated. And not a few have already been savaged and died or disappeared. But even the media, cowered now by constant threats of martial rule and the legalization of warrantless arrests, are slowly closing the door on the truth, marginalizing our dissenting voices in print and in broadcast.

That is why invitations—such as the one you have extended to me—for us to speak out in international solidarity or scholastic meetings such as this one are invaluable to our people. These are very effective vehicles indeed for informing the outside world of the real conditions of people in our land, which is an important task because your support and the concerted solidarity efforts of all our friends abroad help us a long way towards the achievement of genuine peace and freedom in the Philippines.

I believe that most of us here today are already well equipped with sufficient academic and working knowledge of the extent and effects of U.S. military presence in this country. I am therefore going to focus my discussion only on the impact of these bases on our women, as I am well aware that this is one of the least well researched topics relative to this issue. As part of GABRIELA, a national coalition of women's organizations in the Philippines, it is also a subject that is closest to my work and experience.

Nonetheless, let me refresh your memory a little. The United States has a total of twenty-five bases and military installations all over the Philippines, occupying 85,000 hectares of land and 11,000 hectares of waters for their exclusive use. This does not even include a number of installations jointly used by the American and Philippine military. The largest among these installations are Clark Air Base which occupies 55,000 hectares of land in the provinces of Pampanga and Tarlac and Subic Naval Base in neighboring Zambales and Bataan which covers 26,000 hectares of land and 11,000 hectares of its surrounding sea waters. These are also the biggest overseas bases of the United States. The other important American military installations in the Philippines are the San Miguel Naval Communications Station on a 2,896-hectare site also in Zambales, Camp John Hay in Baguio City with an area of 396 hectares, and the 157-hectare Wallace Air Station in La Union. Stationed in these bases are around 16,358 American servicemen. Residing in these areas are an estimated 41,000 American base personnel and their families.

The presence of foreign military bases in the Philippines is a direct encroachment on Philippine affairs and is a blatant insult on our so-called independence. So long as they exist, there is no telling how far and how firmly the United States will intervene and impose its position in our internal affairs. A recent proof to this is the clear visibility and even prominence of U.S. fighter planes during the failed *coup d'état* in December of 1989. So insolent is the attitude of U.S. President George Bush toward our President Aquino that during her Washington visit this year he personally delivered his "No bases,

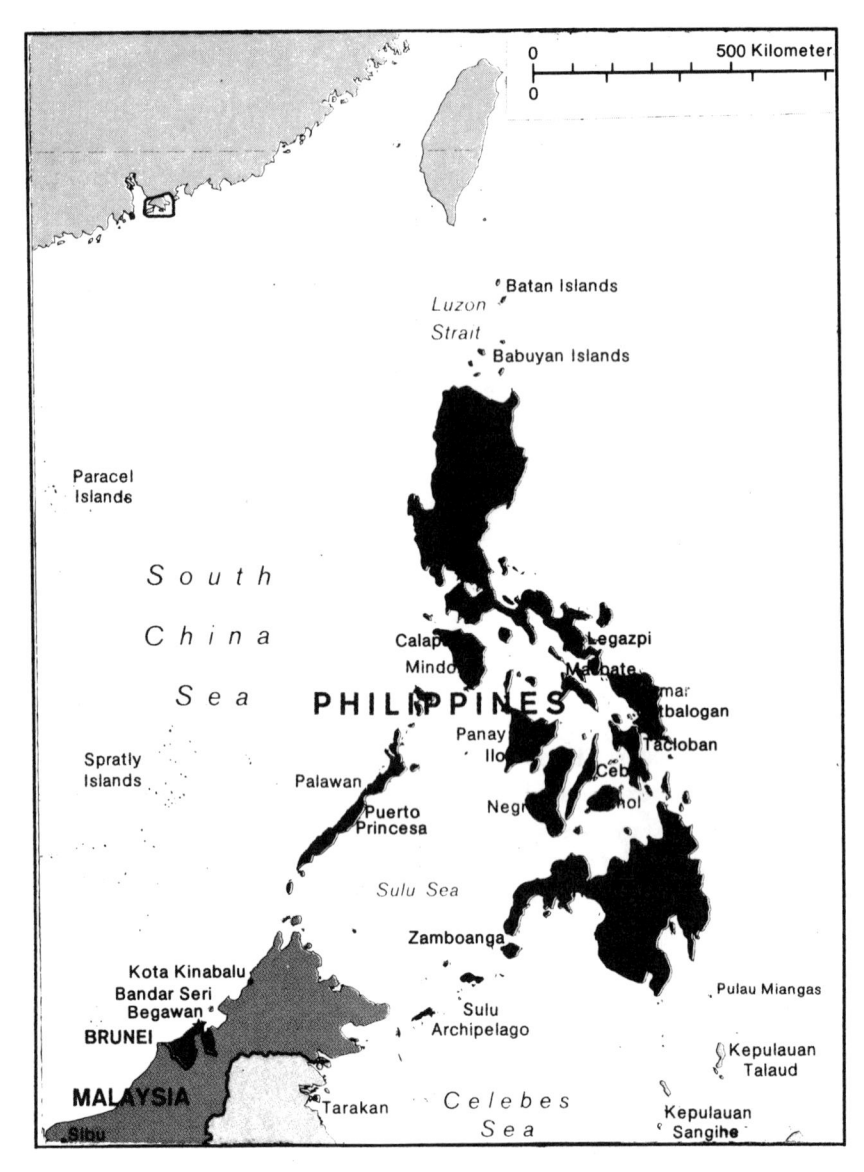

A total of twenty-five U.S. military installations occupy some 85,000 hectares of Philippine territory. Clark Air Base is the largest U.S. base outside of the U.S. and the U.S. is the largest employer after the Philippine government, thus dominating the economy.

no aid" threat, confirming our early analysis tht the Philippine Aid Plan is no sincere effort but a premeditated scheme to press for the extension of the military bases treaty after 1991. Even the shape and direction of our economy has been controlled by American interests which have practically dictated the contents of President Aquino's Memorandum of Economic Policy sent to the International Monetary Fund and the World Bank last year.

In terms of security, the bases actually do not afford us any protection from external threats at all. Such threats are almost non-existent in the first place as the Philippines has no known enemies and is in fact friendly with all other nations, regardless of differences in ideological beliefs. Contrarily, the United States through its bases in the our country, drags us into its own wars of intervention in various parts of the world. Consequently, they open us to military attack or retaliation from American adversaries. At the worst, the whole Filipino nation is now in danger of perishing in a "limited nuclear war" that some U.S. militarists are now apparently willing to undertake when the need arises. This is not yet to mention the effects and possibilities of nuclear accidents within Clark and Subic themselves where evidently nuclear arms are stored in spite of American denials to the contrary.

Scientists have projected that women and children will be the ones who will suffer most in the event of any nuclear explosion. Millions are expected to die instantly. Thousands will die of cancer and other fatal diseases caused by radiation. Likewise, thousands of unborn children will be miscarried and those unfortunate enough to live will most likely carry lifelong infirmities and abnormalities. Even now, in fact, many women living in the peripheries of Clark and Subic have already reported cases of spontaneous abortion, difficulty in childbirth, and malformities in some newborn children as a result of U.S. practice bombing exercises and the noise of low-flying military aircraft in their vicinity. Many mothers in Angeles, particularly, have complained of deafness among their infants.

But perhaps the most tangible and pervasive problem of Filipino women that is directly bases-related is military prostitution. The base cities of Olongapo outside Subic Naval Base and Angeles adjacent to Clark Air Base are witnesses to a flesh trade that has so abnormally grown that the Philippines now bears the degrading notoriety of being the current sex capital in Asia, the favorite of servicemen in the U.S. Seventh Fleet. It must be noted that prior to the establishment of U.S. military bases in Zambales and Pampanga, prostitution was never thought of as a large-scale commercial venture. The demands of U.S. servicemen for rest and recreation, particularly during the Korean and Vietnam wars, have however given rise to numerous prostitution dens in these areas. Embarrassingly, prostitution is now institutionalized as an industry, under the euphemism of Rest and Recreation Industry. Licensed by the Office of Social Hygiene, prostitutes carrying the whitewashed label "hospitality girls" go through dehumanizing acts on-stage and in hotel rooms to satisfy the sexual perversions of American servicemen and international businessmen in search of rest and recreation.

The government's office of Social Hygiene has so far recorded 16,000 hospitality girls in Olongapo and 15,000 in Angeles. In addition, there are more than 3,000 waitresses working as non-registered prostitutes and around 8,000 street-walkers soliciting customers outside bars.

A depressing development in recent years is also the increasing incidence of child prostitution not only in Angeles and Olongapo, but also in other places frequented by foreigners, particularly U.S. servicemen. This includes Bauio City the site of Camp John Hay, La Union the site of the Wallace Air Station, and Ermita in Manila where the U.S. Embassy is located. The youngest recorded or licensed prostitute is only fourteen (14) years old. There are, of course, no official records for child prostitutes roaming the streets. Based on newspaper accounts and academic interviews, however, the youngest noted male and female children sold in the flesh trade are six (6) to seven (7) years old.

Past studies have shown that most women caught in this quagmire of military prostitution hail from very poor peasant families in extremely depressed provinces like Bicol, Samar, and Leyte. In a recent survey conducted by Aida Santos and associate sociologists, however, it appears that an increasing number of women entertainers in the base areas, particularly Angeles, now come from economically better-off

Tagalog speaking provinces. Many now come from working class families, being children of service workers (i.e., drivers, mechanics, carpenters, security guards, etc.).

The prevalent reasons for the women's fall into the flesh trade is still primarily dire economic want. Ironically, however, these women usually find that contrary to myths of easy wealth in prostitution, money in Angeles and Olongapo is not at all that easy to come by. Women entertainers generally work all days of the week for eight or more hours daily. And yet the average earnings of entertainers in bars reach up only to P1,500 per month while street-walkers average P3,000 per month. With the high cost of living in the base cities, moreover, these women normally end up with nothing at all to send their families, for whom most of them have entered the trade in the first place. Ultimately, when a prostitute reaches the age of 30, she is invariably forced to retire and most of them end up even economically worse than when they started—not to mention the destruction of personality and loss of human dignity that they have endured in the hands of men who regard them only as commodities.

Lamentably, the commodification of Filipino women is not at all limited to the base areas. It has also flourished, during recent years, in tourist areas as a result of the government's lopsided development agenda. Preoccupied with raising dollars to pay for our growing debts, the government itself, starting with the Marcos regime, has developed prostitution as a major attraction for Philippine tourism. We are now also exporting our women as mail order brides, domestic helpers, and entertainers (i.e., prostitutes) abroad. The commercialization of women continues to grow even locally due to greater demands for sex shows, pornographic films, and magazines. White female slavery has indeed become a lucrative business for syndicates.

Accompanying the prostitution problem is the issue of sex-related health problems. Sexually transmitted diseases, particularly venereal disease and gonorrhea, have long reached the epidemic proportions in Angeles and Olongapo. This time, it is the killer Acquired Immune Deficiency Syndrome (AIDS) that is causing panic in the base cities. Not indigenous to Filipinos, it is widely believed to have been brought by U.S. servicemen. As of February last year, *Asiaweek* has reported that 70% of 93 people already affected by the disease are found around Clark Air Base and Subic Naval Base. If unchecked, this is expected to triple during the next decade. The sorry reality is, however, that neither the United States nor the Philippine government is doing much to stop the spread of the AIDS virus and other sexually-transmitted diseases among our women. There is practically no way for Filipinos to effectively bar AIDS-infected servicemen and foreigners from coming to the Philippines. Ironically in fact, prostitutes in Angeles

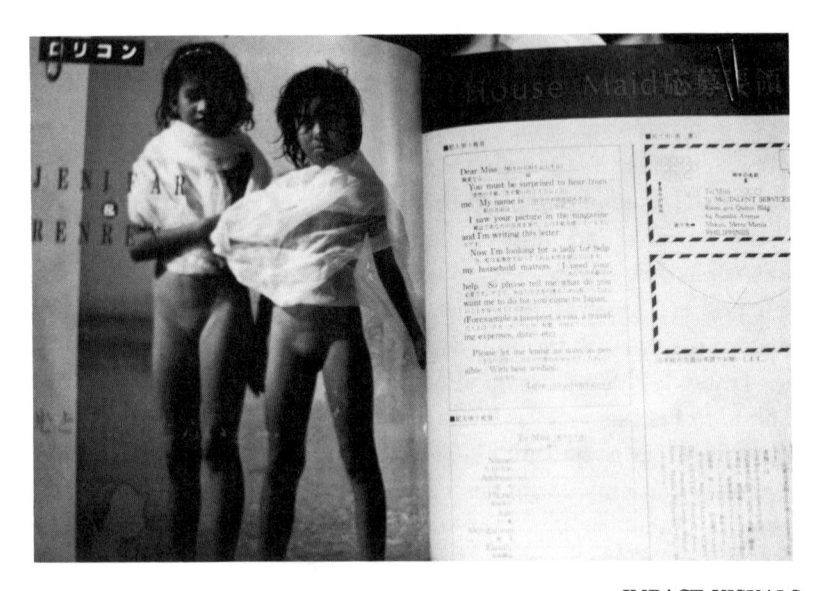

IMPACT VISUALS

This advertisement for mail order Filipina children appeared in a Japanese sex magazine. Placed by Mic Talent Services Center located in Manila, the advertisement claims to be for "House Maids." The fact is that most of these girls sold to Japan or the U.S. end up as prostitutes or sex slaves. Accompanying the photo is a sample letter for "ordering" one of the "maids." It reads,
 "Dear Miss _____.
 You must be surprised to hear from me. My name is _____.
 I saw your picture in the magazine and I'm writing this letter. Now I'm looking for a lady for help [with] my household. I need your help. So please tell me what do you want me to do for you to come to Japan (for example, a passport, a visa, a travelling expense, date . . . etc.). Please let me know as soon as possible. With best wishes!
 Love, _____.

and Olongapo are now required to show their customers medical certificates attesting to their "cleanliness." No such certificates are, of course, required for the customers.

Upon deeper scrutiny, we may also find that sexually transmitted diseases are not the only health hazards rampant in the base areas. Due to lack of nutritious food, excessive work and abuse of their bodies, late nights, and mental as well as psychological strains, women entertainers easily succumb to either common or fatal ailments. Addiction to prohibited drugs is just one of the most common problems.

On the question of abortion, it is an "open secret" in Angeles and Olongapo that its incidence is unchecked, despite the government's declaration that the practice is illegal. It is in fact this very law which endangers the lives of many women and children as the women are forced to go to backstreet quack-doctors charging from 7.76–77.65 pesos for their services, depending on the maturity of the unborn child in the womb. Most of these illegal abortionists use the massage system or utilize catheters and even clothes hangers in their operations. It is therefore not surprising that a large number of women entertainers succumb to post-abortion hemorrhage, infections, and blood poisoning.

Actually, the very poor level of health care among women prostitutes is only a small reflection of the appalling situation of Filipino women's health in general. With the state allocating 40.8% of its national budget to debt repayment and 8.25% to national defense but only 4% to health care, it not only undermines women's rights to adequate health protection, it also heaps upon women's shoulders the burden of their families' health needs.

Because of state neglect and for many of our poor even outright denial of adequate health protection for women, there is a very high maternal mortality rate in the Philippines even outside abortion malpractices. The immediate causes for these are usually hemorrhage, infection, and hypertension—all reflections of inadequate prenatal care and unattended deliveries. Malnutrition due to extreme poverty in the country, heavy workloads, double burden of work, and lack of education about their own bodies all add up to many women's vulnerability to death at childbirth and even during the child-rearing period.

Aside from these catastrophic health problems, an offshoot of prostitution around the U.S. military bases is the ballooning population of street-children, most of whom are Amerasians, meaning the offspring of American servicemen and their Filipina entertainers. Known as "souvenir babies," these children are invariably unwanted and are a source of additional worries for their mothers. Consequently, many of them are left on their own in the streets or are sold at bargain prices as low as $25 to $200 depending on their racial origin and physical attributes. Not a few, however, are trained to be second-generation prostitutes by their own parents. Without the birth of one Amerasian every day—the highest incidence in Asia—there would not be about 35,000 Amerasian street-kids in the base areas.

The other group of women immediately affected by U.S. military presence is of course those who have been displaced from their ancestral lands by the coming of the Americans. These are primarily the tribal women—the Aetas in Zambales and the Igorots in Benguet, site of Camp John Hay. Together with their families, they have been marginalized and driven into the mountain areas where they have to survive on meager forest resources. Others have settled as squatters in their own land, living in shanties around the base peripheries, scavenging for crumbs and scrap materials from the base areas.

Scavenging around and in the bases, however, has become very dangerous ever since the American authorities decided to bury their wastes rather than allow the poor Filipino to salvage what they can from such garbage. Some American servicemen have taken to shooting people like wild boars, letting their police dogs attack children, and sexually molesting, even raping, women whom they have caught poaching in "American territory." The saddest part in all these, however, is that such crimes committed by American soldiers are not, and by US-RP agreements could not, be tried in Philippine courts. While U.S. officials claim that these cases get elevated to American courts, most if not all of the culprits are normally allowed to go scot free.

Finally, it is also mainly the Filipino woman's travail that Angeles and Olongapo have also become centers of vices such as gambling, smuggling, black marketing, extortion, and drug trafficking, thereby creating a very dim future for their children. Already, many mothers

Robert Gumpert / IMPACT VISUALS

residing in these areas have been harassed by their children who have fallen victim to these vices. Easy prey for drug pushers in Olongapo and Angeles are young boys and girls trying to adopt the carousing life-style of American servicemen. As early as 1982, a survey already revealed that 80% of Olongapo's high school boys were using dangerous drugs. A similar survey the next year showed that 80% likewise of the city's street-children were addicted to rugby solvent, an acetone mixture, sniffed like glue.

In addition, drug dealers widely use children to retail their goods. A whole army of kids is involved now in the sale of narcotics. Many of them residing in the squatter colonies near the bases, their families have accepted the situation because sometimes it represents their families' only incomes. In some cases, drug dealers rent houses where rooms similar to traditional hop joints are maintained for clients. These houses are frequently guarded by armed youths. Spending six to seven hours in such a house, a boy could net $10 to $200 for risking arrest.

Aside from all these, the presence of military bases in the country has also given growth to the crime rate in their host provinces and municipalities. Day to day, therefore, and in fact minute to minute, women and children have to live with the threat of violence and the sudden curtailment of their lives.

Considering therefore that women and children figure among the hardest hit by the continued presence of U.S. military bases in this country, with tens of thousands already caught in the quagmire of prostitution and distorted social mores affecting the base peripheries, the women of GABRIELA strongly demand the immediate removal of all U.S. military facilities in our land. We oppose any negotiation for their continued stay in the Philippines after the 1947 US-RP Military Bases Agreement expires next year. Moreover, we expect a genuine national socio-economic development after complete American pull-out.

It is in this spirit that the GABRIELA National Women's Coalition, in complete unity with all other people-based organizations working for a bases-free and nuclear-free Philippines, declared last year, on the 27th day of October, its visions for an alternative life without U.S. bases in the Philippines.

The Plight Of The Kanak People In New Caledonia

Susanna Ounei

Our workshop during the Pacific Policy Congress began with participants sharing their knowledge of the Kanak struggle. For the majority, attention had only been drawn to Kanaky in 1987. I then gave a background to the present Kanak struggle. The Kanak people own no land. When the French took possession of the islands, all the land was taken over by the State which subsequently made grants to individual settlers and allocated areas for Kanak reserves. Every new settler who comes into New Caledonia is subsidized by the French Government and can take the land. The Caldoche (French/mixed race settlers and New Caledonian born) have all the money and power. No Kanak has any power. Kanaks fill unskilled laboring positions or are unemployed. They do not receive social security benefits.

Susanna Ounei was one of the first Kanak women activists to travel internationally to represent the FLNKS (Front de Libération National Kanak et Socialistè). Like many other Third World women, her position has been primarily to pose the struggle of Kanak women for equality and justice within the framework of national liberation for all Kanak people in New Caledonia, not just an organizing effort by women for themselves. Currently living in New Zealand with her peace activist husband, David Small, Susanna continues to inform Pacific people about the situation in that country. — Angela Gilliam

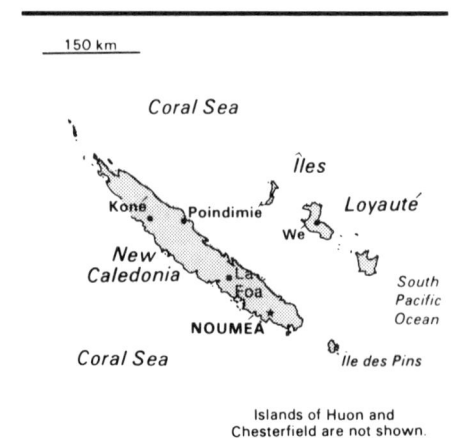

New Caledonia - Kanaky
Overseas territory of France. Population, 153,215: 42% Melanesian Kanaks, 37% European, Wallisian 8%, Polynesian 4%, Vietnamese 2%. Total area, 19,060.

There is a long-standing feeling of powerless among the Kanaks and because they speak little or no English, they are isolated from the rest of the peoples of the Pacific. In 1990, the Kanaks numbered 73,000 out of a total population of 175,000. Kanaks are a minority in their own country. When referenda are held on independence, the vote is lost 3-2.

New Caledonia was colonized by the French in 1853. There were approximately 75,000 Kanaks at that time. Many Kanaks were eliminated and the rest were removed from their land and moved into the less fertile hills. Until 1946 Kanaks were not permitted to enter Nouméa or any white areas; if they did they would be shot or expelled. The French brought in people from Wallis and Futuna, Tahiti, and Vietnam—that is from the other French territories. Kanaks were used as slave labor to build roads, pick coffee, and perform other kinds of labor in support of French colonizers.

Aotearoa had a treaty; Polynesia had a protectorate; the Kanaks had nothing. Since 1853, there has been fighting and resistance, but it was always isolated. 1878 saw the first national uprising organized by Kanak chiefs and warriors. Women were involved, taking responsibility for the children and the old people, while the men fought. The second national uprising occurred in 1917. During this time the chief was beheaded and thousands of Kanaks were killed. Again, the women took part in the uprising.

Traditionally, when women married, they took land into the marriage and responsibility for children was shared. The extended family played an important role. The influence of the French has

Susanna Ounei, Presidente du Groupa des Femmes Kanak en Lutte

had a detrimental effect on Kanak family life. For example, the ideas of extra-marital affairs and flirting were brought to Kanaky by the French. Today, many marriages break-up and women are left alone with the responsibility of raising their children. Many women are the victims of domestic violence, induced in part by the depressed state of their men, and women are choosing to live as single parents to avoid physical abuse. But the result is also the breaking of tradition and the destruction of culture.

The French policy was one of complete assimilation. All citizens of New Caledonia are supposed to be French, but not all citizens have the same rights. Kanaks have few rights and are at the bottom of the heap. "Kanak" simply means "man belonging to the land." There are over twenty-seven languages spoken by different groups of Kanaks.

In 1969, Nidoish Naisseline, the son of a grandchief from Mare returned to New Caledonia from France where he had received an education. He was the first to do so. Up until this time, many people had been ashamed to identify themselves as Kanak. Naisseline, a founding member of Palika, wrote pamphlets in Kanak for which he was arrested and sent back to France for three months. In 1972, Naisseline was arrested again for writing in Kanak. This time he was sentenced to six months in prison.

After 1946, Unione Caledonia (UC) was formed with membership of white French and Kanak elders. UC is the largest political party in FLNKS (Front de Libération National et Socialiste). Its members focused on issues of justice and human rights, but at this time there was no talk of independence. By 1969, a restored a feeling of identity among the Kanaks had emerged. In 1977, the UC adopted a pro-independence policy.

From the 1988 disturbances, there has been pressure for the U.N. to put New Caledonia on the de-colonization list. The fear for the French is that if New Caledonia goes, then French Polynesia goes and that puts an end to French testing of nuclear weapons in the Pacific. The French have been buying off other Pacific nations with negotiations for bi-lateral aid. Fourteen million dollars was given to Fiji. Consequently, some Pacific nations will not vote against France in the United Nations on issues of nuclear testing and independence. However, there is strong pressure from other island states for Kanak independence spearheaded by Papua New Guinea, Vanuatu, and the Solomon Islands.

The main purpose for continued French colonial control of New Caledonia appears to be the military strategy. There seems to be little economic advantage for France hanging on to New Caledonia since 93% of the island's economy derives from France and only 30% of the income from tourism stays in the country. There are vast mineral reserves but these haven't been developed.

The discussion then turned to the history of Kanak Resistance. It was pointed out that there had always been Kanak resistance, but it was isolated. In 1979, on Ouvéa, Kanaks burnt down the tourist resorts. In 1984, FLNKS was founded as a coalition of political parties and human rights groups. In 1988, the Congress Kanak Socialist Liberation Front began an active boycott. On Ouvéa, what began as a peaceful protest resulted in the death of six French and nineteen Kanaks. It was never intended that hostages be taken, but during the two weeks that they were held in the cave they were well cared for by the Kanak people. The Kanak leaders wanted to negotiate with the president but not with the army. The army retaliated by harassing the women and children. Any known activists were also harassed by the army.

In June 1988, President Tjabaou was called to France in order to work out some resolution to the growing independence movement. FLNKS asked that only Caldoche (i.e., citizens with at least one parent born in New Caledonia) and Kanaks be allowed to vote in the independence referendum. But rather than permit an immediate vote, the Matignon Accords were signed with the French Government and Jacques Lafleur, the right wing leader of the Caldoche community. The Accords were ratified in a referendum in November 1988, but 43% of the population opposed them.

The Matignon Accords stated that there would be direct rule from Paris until 14th July, 1989. In June, elections would be held for three provincial Governments. A referendum on independence would not be held until 1998. Under the Matignon Accords, the French

Government was to establish a separate electoral roll and a system of monitoring the eligibility of those listed. Those eligible to vote in the 1998 referendum would be those on the electoral roll for the 1988 referendum and their children who reached voting age before 1998. One requirement for eligibility was that a person must have lived continuously in New Caledonia.

The 1972 Nessmmer Amendment had encouraged immigration from France in order to a make majority of New Caledonians white. The game of the French government was to divide the people. Since 1987, there have been 4,500 new immigrants. As of this date, the electorate has not been defined nor is there any method of monitoring continuous residency. New immigrants are permitted to vote after only six months residency. The French Government has been actively lobbying at the United Nations to have New Caledonia removed from the UN de-colonization list, saying that the problems have been solved by the Matignon Accords. The Matignon Accords, however, make no attempt to dismantle colonial structures, but rather reinforce patterns which handicap Kanak development. France is not acknowledging and implementing its obligations under the UN resolution 1514 to prepare the population to progress toward independence. The Matignon Accords do not correspond to the UN requirements and do NOT guarantee Kanak independence.

Kanaks need self-determination and independence. They also need understanding by the rest of the world. Unfortunately, some books such as Helen Fraser's book, published in 1982, are grossly inaccurate. Better resources are books by Michael Spencer, Alan Ward, and John Connell, *New Caledonia: Essays in Nationalism and Dependency*. Also very important are the books by Myriam Dornoy Vurobaravu, *Politics in New Caledonia* and Ingrid Kirchner, *The Kanaks of New Caledonia*.

At the conclusion of the workshop all participantts agreed to the following resolution: That New Caledonia be given priority on the UN de-colonization list.

The System Of National Accounts, Or The Measure and Mis-Measure Of Value And Production In Economic Theory

Marilyn Waring

Let me begin with three stories. In 1976, when I was a very young Member of the New Zealand Parliament, a South African based company applied for a mining license on Mount Pirongia, a Forest Park in my old constituency. Leaving aside the obvious politics of the company's country of origin, the company was able to demonstrate in its application that mining would create economic growth. Employment would be created and provided, the local business community and surrounding rural infrastructure would benefit from the flow-on effects of that employment, government taxation revenue would flow, and the nation's export earnings would be boosted. All these claims were projected in monetary terms.

At the local community level it was obvious to us that Mount

Editor's Note—Marilyn Waring, a leading feminist economist, served as a Member of parliament in New Zealand's National Government. In 1984, her advocacy of a nuclear-free New Zealand brought about the fall of the Muldoon government. The author of *If Women Counted*, she holds a doctorate in political economy and is opening up new vistas in feminist economics which challenge the repressive patriarchal economics of capitalism.

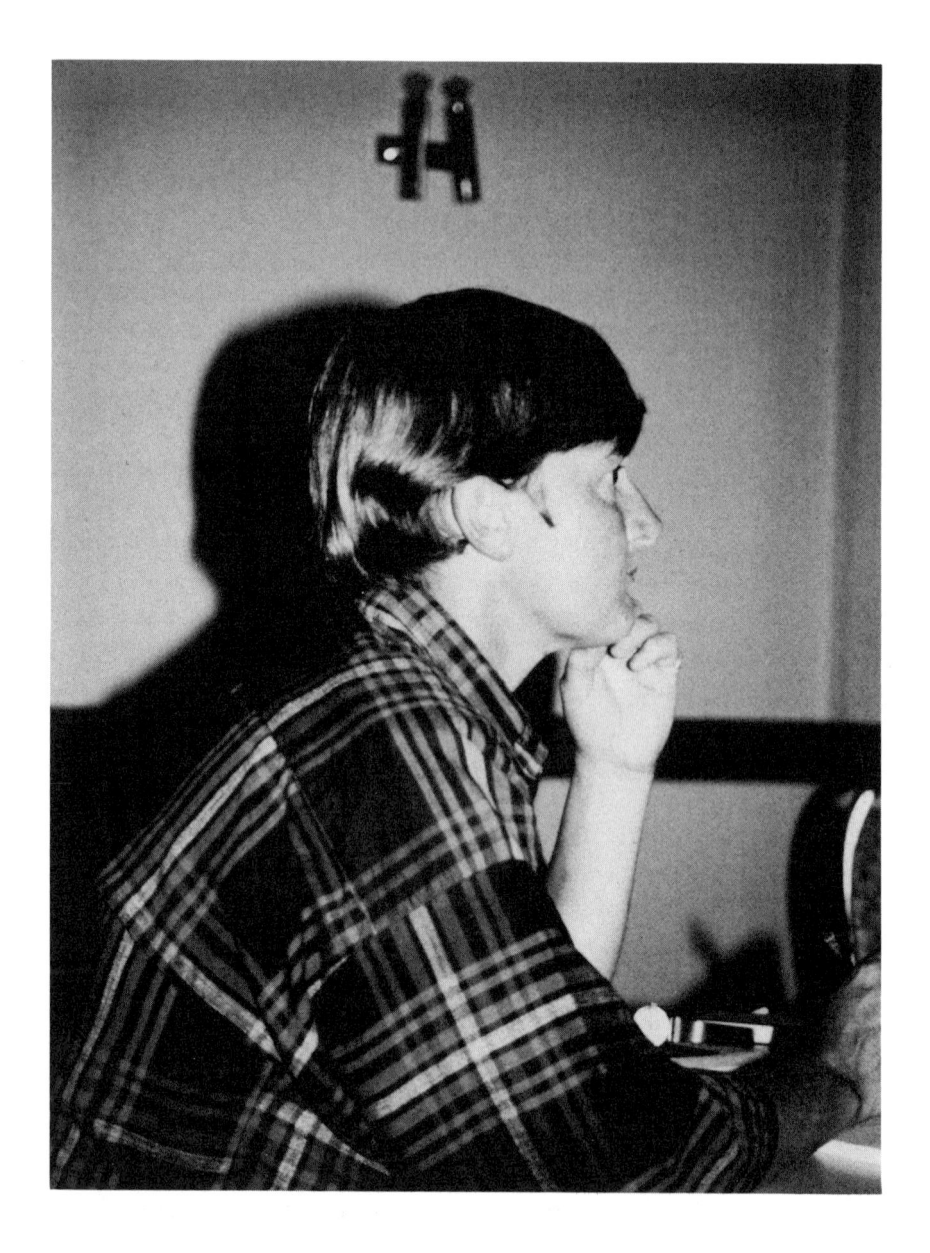

Marilyn Waring

Pirongia already played a major role in our lives. It was a feature of a climate that sustained the richest dairy farm area in the country. The forest breathed—it provided oxygen. The trees helped to sustain water table levels. The forest was a habitat for all the pollinating and seeding agents vital for a good agricultural balance and was home as well to a number of endangered species. And many of us loved to hike and tramp the steep, sweet smelling paths. Oh yes, there were economic models which could have calibrated a monetary value for all these activities, but why, we asked, should we be forced to resort to such a crude tool to assert a "value." But that's what we would have been left with, had Mount Pirongia not been the source of domestic water supply for the nearby town of Te Awamutu, and that was the deciding feature of the argument.

To another, very short, story. On a coral atoll in the Pacific, in an area where the French still insist that their nuclear testing has no effect on the food chain, women go through what seems, at first, to be a strange ritual when they are preparing to process fresh fish. They hang them on a line, as if they were laundry, for a very short time. They watch carefully and if any flies land on a fish, they quickly take it down. After a short period of time, fish are left that even the flies avoid. These contaminated specimens are discarded. Only those that attract the flies are still safe for human consumption.

Now let's examine the voyage of the *Exxon Valdez*. Had the tanker loaded its fuel and had an uneventful voyage, a moderate amount of market exchange would have occurred to add to the Alaskan and U.S. gross national product. That moderation pales into insignificance with the market exchange possible when a captain manages to lose his ship and cargo. There is the need for a new tanker, insurance pay-outs, the legal, criminal, environmental, and civil prosecutions, compensation to fisherpersons and others whose livelihoods were affected, salaries for those involved in the inefficient clean up, the media spectacle, the films, books, videos, plays, movies, the boost in membership to environmental organizations and the parade of other money consequences. This was one of the most valuable oil tanker excursions in history. There is no debit side to national income accounting; all of that expenditure is recorded as growth.

What does remain invisible in the *Exxon Valdez* case is the ongoing damage to the ecosystem and the environment. Did sea birds, sea lions, and the ruination of an ecological chain generate economic consequences? For the purposes of national income accounting, the majority of people on the planet are as the sea lions and the sea birds. Growth figures do not measure the extent of poverty, the distribution of poverty, the quality of life or the well being of a population despite the fact that almost every politician and every economist you run into will claim that they care.

This inquiry into macro-economics began when from 1975 to 1984 I was appointed to, and then chaired, the Public Expenditure Select Committee (which is the public accounts/appropriations/budget committee) of the New Zealand Parliament. At one point of my tenure in the chair, New Zealand revised its System of National Accounts in accordance with changes suggested by the United Nations. Treasury wheeled up this machinery piece of legislation and said we want this bill to go through next week, can you pop it through the committee? I had already been chairing the committee for three years, yet I had never heard of the System of National Accounts. It was then that I underwent a rude awakening as to what they were. I learned that in this United Nations System of National Accounts (UNSNA) the things that I valued most about life in my country—its pollution free environment, its mountain streams with safe drinking water, the accessibility of national parks, walkways, beaches, lakes, and beach forest, the total absence of nuclear power and nuclear energy—all counted for nothing. They weren't counted for in private consumption expenditure, general government expenditure, gross domestic capital formation. Nuclear bombs are counted, by the way, not in New Zealand, but in other places. Yet, these accounting systems were used to determine all public policies. Since the environment effectively counted for nothing there couldn't be any value on policy measures that would ensure its preservation. Hand in hand with the dismissal of the environment came evidence of the severe invisibility of women and women's work. For example, as a politician, I found it virtually impossible for me to prove, given the production framework in which we were placed, that child care facilities were needed. Non-producers, housewives, mothers who are inactive and unoccupied—that is, not measurably productive or occupied—cannot apparently be in need. They are not even in the economic cycle in the first place; they can certainly have no expectation that they be visible in the distribution of benefits that flow from production.

These injustices result from this System of National Accounts. We are more familiar with hearing words like gross domestic product, gross national product, growth—all figures which are derivative from the SNA. It is an international system of economic measurement. Every country is required to use it and every country is required to use exactly the same rules for any annual report recognized by the World Bank, the International Monetary Fund, United Nations Agencies or statistics of national governments. The U.N. uses the accounts to access annual contributions to appraise the success of regional development programs. Aid donors use national accounts to identify deserving cases. Need is apparently determined by per capita gross domestic product. The World Bank uses these figures to identify nations that most urgently need economic assistance. Multinational corporations use the same figures to locate new areas for overseas investments and companies predict markets for their goods on the basis of national accounts projections and plan their investment personnel and other internal policies.

For individual countries the use made of national accounts and their supporting statistics are manifold and have far reaching effects. They are used to create frameworks and models for the integration of economic statistics generally. They are used to analyze past and current developments in the national economy. They are the basis for predictions of the possible effects of any change within policy or any other economic changes. They are used to quantify all areas of what is considered the national economy so that resource allocations can be made accordingly. Governments project public service requirements and revenue requirements for the nations, plan new construction, training and other programs necessary to meet these needs all by using the national accounts. They are used to forecast short and medium term trends; they are also used internationally to compare one nation's performance to another.

Chapter II
BASIC CONCEPTS

1. Introduction

The aim of national accounting is to describe the structure of an economic system in terms of transactions. Production may be taken as a basic concept and section 2 of this chapter is devoted to a definition of the value of production. Production in this broad sense is subdivided according to its uses and the main distinctions in this respect are set out in section 3. So far the concepts defined relate to products and their valuation. In section 4 the finance of the expenditure on these products is considered and is traced back to its ultimate source either in domestic productive activity or in the rest of the world. By setting out the matter in this way a complete description is given of the transactions in an economic system. It is apparent, however, that when this stage has been reached great advantages accrue from presenting the network of transactions in terms of a system of accounts. This is done in section 5.

2. The definition of the value of production

(a) The boundary of production

Production is a basic concept which can be described as the provision of goods and services. Not all production, however, in this broad sense is included in the concept of economic production. It is, therefore, necessary to state as clearly as possible the line of distinction between production that is, and production that is not included. This may be done conveniently by drawing a production boundary and, accordingly, the object of this section is to explain how this should be done.

In a monetary economy all goods and services included in the concept of production if they changed for money. However, it is obv... summation of commodities ... would result in a measu... actions or turnov... unduplicated some...

---

stocks) of all producers and to deduct from this total the purchases of these producers from other producers, the intermediate products referred to in the last paragraph. A net figure of this kind can be obtained for each producer separately and represents the value added by him to the value of the intermediate products with which he starts and hence his contribution to the total value of production. Looked at from a different point of view this value added represents the wages, profits and other forms of income that accrue in productive activity.

The second method is suggested by the fact that in the above calculation of net outputs, the value of all intermediate products appears positively as the output of one producer and negatively as the input of another producer. As a consequence all intermediate products may be cancelled out and the value of total production be obtained by summing all final products as defined above.

These ways of deriving the total value of production are equivalent but their subdivision leads to three distinct classifications of this total. Aggregate value added may be subdivided to show the portion of total production originating in various form of organization or by ...producti... gories. The income shares ...ork...in... added may be recon... each type of ... the to...

Basic Concepts

...then separating two types of purchases by enterprises, namely those which are and those which are not charged to current cost. The boundary is drawn around the production accounts of enterprises which contain all sales but only the purchases of enterprises which are charged to current expense. Sales which are not so charged flow across the boundary to households or to the capital accounts of enterprises and are final product. Sales which are so charged begin and end within the boundary and are intermediate product.

The distinction between enterprises and households is not in all cases sufficient to draw a satisfactory production boundary. In the simplest case, households may buy direct services, such as domestic services, from other households and it seems reasonable to regard these services as part of production. This can be done by recognizing a limited amount of production within households. The household that buys the direct services rendered by other households is thought of as buying at cost, in its capacity as a consumer, the direct services from a production account to which is debited the cost of the services. This production account, like any other, lies within the production boundary and what flows out of it is part of final product.

In addition to this case, in which households render direct services to each other, the separation of transactors into households and enterprises raises problems because of the existence of many other examples of households engaging in activities which it seems reasonable to regard as a part of production. For instance, farm households are not only households from the consuming point of view but also enterprises which engage in agricultural production. These two aspects of their activity must be separated and this may be done by setting up a production account to which purchases and sales in respect of their productive activity are debited and credited and a consumption account to which is credited their income and to which is debited their consumption expenditure. These households usually produce agricultural products for their own consumption as well as for the market and it is desirable to impute a sale by their production account to their consumption account in respect of the value of the produce which they consume. It will be evident that the costs incurred in producing output for home consumption will have to be debited to the production account in the same manner as the costs incurred in producing for the market. Consequently, the net profit shown on the debit side of the production account and transferred to the net return on marketing a net ...lude in addition to ... ...ome consumed output.

under-developed countries, however, the reverse is the case and so it is important to set up clearly defined rules for drawing the production boundary.

The following rules have as their object the inclusion in production of household activities that are clearly akin to those which are usually undertaken in enterprises and the exclusion of those for which the analogy with enterprises becomes tenuous and which do not lend themselves to any precise definition. It is convenient in stating these rules to draw a distinction between primary and other producers.

In the case of primary producers, that is those engaged in agriculture, forestry, hunting, fishing, mining and quarrying, all primary production whether exchanged or not and all other goods and services produced and exchanged are included in the total of production. In the case of other producers, that is, those engaged in all other industries listed in the *International Standard Industrial Classification*, the total of their primary production is included as for primary producers. In addition there is included the total of their other production which is exchanged together with the unexchanged part of their production in their own trade. As a result of these rules there is omitted from production the net amount of all non-primary production performed by producers outside their own trades and consumed by themselves. Non-primary production may be defined broadly as the transformation and distribution of tangible commodities as well as the rendering of services.

These rules are in close agreement with the imputation procedures used for industrialized economies. The farming imputation made for such economies accords with the rules given for primary producers and the rental imputation accords with the rules given for other producers if account is taken of the fact that home-ownership is regarded as a trade. In practice, no other imputations of this kind are made since primary production and the consumption of their own produce by non-primary producers is of little or no importance.

The existence of government activity gives rise to further problems in drawing the production boundary and these are solved in exactly the same way as for households. Government engages in selling and producing activities analogous to those which take place in business enterprises and these activities are separated from those of the general government by setting up production accounts for them. General government activities are treated like the activities of households. The hiring of the direct services provided by civil servants and members of the armed forces involves the setting up of a production account as in the case of ...tion by general govern-

---

From A System of National Accounts and Supporting Tables, (United Nations, 1953). Work done for the purpose of human sustenance is carefully excluded from the national economy. Only work done for monetary profit is important to the health and well being of a nation.

Economic historians say that the national income system can probably be traced to the Doomsday book, but there has always been a hidden political motive or a political need for any country to establish national income accounts. Euphemisms such as mercantile expansionism are used by political economists to obscure the fact that the accounts have evolved to justify paying for wars. Since the institutionalization of national income accounting by the United Nations in 1953, however, the motive has expanded. The key feature of the United Nations System is derived directly from a pamphlet published in the United Kingdom in 1939 by Sir Richard Stone, the man who won the Nobel Prize for inventing this system, and John Maynard Keynes and James Mead. The full title of the pamphlet is "The British National Income and How To Pay for the War." What the pamphlet is concerned with is demonstrating, for example, that it is much more productive to turn silk into parachutes than into stockings, to turn steel into tanks than into sinks. The motive these days for national income accounting has expanded. A major reason that only cash-generating activities are taken into account is to ensure that countries can determine balance of payments and loan requirements, not as a comparative exercise but as a controlling exercise. Those to whom money is owed—first world governments, multinational banks, multilateral agencies—now impose this system on those who owe them money. They are interested only in seeing the cash-generating capacity.

Whatever the change of motive, two things are constant: those who are making the decisions are men and those values which are excluded from this determination are those of our environment and of women and children. Consider Tendai, a young girl in the Lowveld in Zimbabwe. Her day starts at four a.m. when to fetch water she carries a thirty litre tin to a bore hole about eleven kilometers from her home. She walks bare-footed and she is home by nine a.m. She eats a little and she proceeds to fetch firewood until midday. She cleans the utensils from the family's morning meal and sits preparing a lunch of sadza for the family. After the lunch and the cleaning of the dishes, she wanders in the sun fetching wild vegetables for supper until she makes the same evening trip for water. Her day ends at nine p.m. after she has prepared supper and put her younger brothers and sisters to sleep. According to the System of National Accounts, Tendai is considered unproductive, unoccupied and economically inactive. Tendai does not work and is not part of the labor force and thus produces no value.

Wenche, a young middle class Norwegian housewife spends her day preparing food, setting the table, serving meals, clearing food and dishes from the table, washing dishes, dressing her children, disciplining children and taking the children to daycare and to school, disposing of the garbage, dusting, gathering the clothes for the washing, doing the laundry, going to the gas station or the supermarket, repairing household items, ironing, keeping an eye on or playing with the children, making beds, paying bills, caring for pets and plants, putting away toys, books and clothes, sewing or mending or knitting, talking to door-to-door salespeople, answering the telephone, vacuuming, sweeping, washing the floors, cutting the grass, weeding, and shovelling snow, cleaning the bathroom and kitchen and putting her children to bed. Wenche has to face the fact that she fills her time in a totally unproductive manner; she is economically inactive and economists record her as unoccupied.

Ben is a highly trained member of the U.S. Military. His regular duty is to descend to an underground facility where he waits with a colleague for hours at a time for an order to fire a nuclear missile. So skilled and effective is Ben, that if his colleagues were to attempt to subvert an order to fire, Ben would, if all else failed, be expected to kill them to ensure a successful missile launch. But most of his time is filled with idleness and mindless repetition of training exercises. His work has value and contributes as part of the nuclear machine to the nation's growth, wealth, and productivity. That is what the international economic system says.

Mario is a pimp and a heroin addict in Rome. He regularly pays graft. While Mario's services and his consumption and production are illegal, they are nonetheless marketed. Money changes hands. So, Mario's activities are part of Italy's hidden economy. But in a nation's bookkeeping not all transactions are accounted for. So, a government Treasury or a Reserve bank at the end of any year has the capacity to measure the money legitimately exchanged in the market, and the cash in circulation, and there is a difference. That difference can tell you what the current percentage of the market is in terms of the illegal activity. So, Mario's illegal services and production and consumption activities are recognized and recorded. Mario is a valuable worker; that is what the international economic system says.

Ben and Mario work, Wenche and Tendai do not—those are the rules. I believe that women all over the world with lives as diverse as Wenche and Tendai are economically productive. I imagine most of you, too, think that these women work full days rather than spend them at leisure. But according to the theory, science provision, practice and institutionalization of economics, we are wrong.

The current state of the world then is the result of a system that attributes little or no value to peace; it pays no heed to the preservation of national resources or to the labor of the majority of its inhabitants or to the unpaid work of the reproduction of human life itself, not to mention its maintenance and care. This system cannot respond to values it refuses to recognize.

In his book *Economics in Perspective*, John Kenneth Galbraith condemns the separation of economics from politics as sterile. It is, he says, "A cover for the reality of economic power and motivation, a prime source of misjudgment and error in economic policy." His fundamental thesis is that economic ideas are always and intimately a product of their own time and place. In Galbraith's view, mainstream economics remains an ideological defence of the capitalist system, "A resort and occupation of some of the most determined minds" is how he phrases it. "Not the least of the factors encouraging that," he writes, "is the approval and the income it evoked and still evokes from those who benefit from what is defended." What he does not name and what any school (left or right) of economics remains is an ideological defence of patriarchy.

Most propositions of economics are explained and illustrated by using words—arithmetic, geometry and algebra—these all seem to be ultimate languages which are translatable into each other. Mathematical formulas assist the illusion that economics is a value free science; propaganda is much less easily discerned from figures than it is from words. The process of "theorizing" takes place when economists reason about simplified models of an actual economy or some part of an economy. From this model again "factual predictions" are made. Clearly if you don't perceive the major part of your community as being economically active, they are not in your model and your "correct conclusions" and your "factual predictions" based on the model simply won't include them.

The belief that value results only when (predominantly) men interact within the market place means that few attempts are made to disguise this myopic approach. The power described as operative in the System of National Accounts is patriarchal power. The concept of power embraced in the search for alternatives to the national accounts is undeniably feminist.

Let's look for a moment now at the nature of growth. With but a few admitted problems, the system of national income accounting is thought of as the basic description and analysis of the global economic activity, as witnessed in the series of books titled *State of the World* brought out by Lester Brown and the World Watch Institute in Washington, D.C. National income is recorded arithmetically according to basic accounting rules. The majority of the data is collected primarily for accounting purposes. Sales and purchases, payments and receipts, assets and liabilities visible and recorded in the market are the key sources for such figures. You collect all of these figures for something else and then you crunch them into the framework of national income accounting. Growth in national accounting terms measured in gross national product or gross domestic product includes not only all market transitions including those for armaments, poisons, chemicals, pollutants and other activities normally identified, but also the black market and illegal activities including drug trafficking, prostitution, trading children, pornography, graft and corruption.

The first U.N. publication of the System of National Accounts stated that "the main impetus for the development was the practical need for information about the working of the economic system as a whole and the ways in which the various parts relate to each other," so the aim of the system was that it would offer economic explanations about the way the world would work.

Now "as a whole" implies for me—though, clearly not for the designers—all human beings, as well as all natural resources and even so-called acts of God. The report explained "while national accounting information is useful in all fields of economic decisions making because of the factual background it provides, its outstanding use has been in connection with public policy." This is a key phrase, both in terms of the motivation of the system's authors and in the terms of the system's fallacies. If national accounting provides "factual information"—and that is debatable—then facts are already selected, and they are highly selected in a way that predetermines public policy. The information isn't collected for what it might teach us, but it is collected to further the aims for which the methodology was devised.

It is not as if the motive has been concealed. In the essay "Lessons of the British War Economy," author of the System of National Accounts, Richard Stone, discusses how the economy can be made to function "more in accordance with contemporary social ideas." Powerful men determine what those participant observer contemporary social ideas are. With minor structural changes, the System of National Accounts has remained conceptually intact since 1953, so when international reports and writers refer to women as statistically or economically invisible it is the System of National Accounts that makes it so. When it dawns on you that militarism and destruction of the environment are recorded as growth, the System of National Accounts makes it so. When you are seeking out the most vicious tools of colonization, those that can obliterate a culture, cultural practices, or even a nation, a tribe or a people's value system, then rank the System of National Accounts among them. And when you yearn for a breath of nature's fresh air or a glass of radioactive free water, remember that the System of National Accounts says that both are worthless.

Despite the claim to wholeness and other inter-relatedness the System of National Accounts has decided that certain areas of human activity lie outside a "production boundary." The rules state "the producing and consuming entities in the economy can be exhaustively and exclusively classified as either enterprises or households, and producers can be identified in the former category." The exception to the general rule that production is not found in households is made for rural households provided the main occupation of the head of the household is in primary production. If he works off the farm and he is an accountant for example, it is not a farm household. A housewife by definition cannot be a primary producer; in fact, she can't be any kind of producer. This exclusion is amazing. It says all of these men can be producers, but housework is specifically excluded. Then too, housework is nowhere defined. That makes it possible for housework to become the generic category for absolutely everything that women can do in an unpaid capacity.

So, a housewife cannot be a primary producer and she can't be any kind of producer. She may be agriculturally productive, but her primary role as the provider of household services is specifically excluded from the System of National Accounts. Even when and if the production boundary is extended to include non-monetary activities, building, construction, processing, storage, transportation, the carriage of water, collection of firewood, subsistence crop production, the work performed by women is still excluded because women are housewives.

The United Nations System of National Accounts is quite clear about women. In no uncertain terms it tells us, "Primary production and the consumption of their own produce by other than non-primary producers is of little or no importance." I object! It just feeds the world. It just keeps people alive. It just sustains households. It just makes it possible for everyone else to go to work. It just reproduces human beings. The failure of the United Nations, the International Labor Organization, and all governments is symptomatic of a willingness to obscure all voluntary, community, and other altruistic work, and all unpaid rural work, and food storage, and food processing, and primary health care work as housework.

It is also demonstrative of the political power and myopia of the power brokers' participant observation. Men who make the rules don't do housework. Men who make the rules couldn't list all the categories if they spent years at it. It is simpler and has ensured a slave caste to name all of this production and consumption as unoccupied economic inactivity. Despite the fact that the household is both the center of consumption and the supplier of all factors of consumption, they say it is not a family operated enterprise. This is in spite of the fact that the realistic observation that much household consumption can also be seen as productivity, increasing investments in the health, education, and nutrition of the household's human capital.

In reality, economic production covers the whole range of human activities devoted to the creation with limited resources of goods and services capable of satisfying human wants. The system claims to provide essential background for public policy formation but the inability to attribute a market value to unpaid functions does not mean that a place cannot be found for them in the public policy equation, and yet when such a place is found it is generally termed "welfare." In a similar way no account is taken of costs to human health and to the availability of basic needs by the degradation of the ecosystem, all usually recorded as growth. Nor is account taken of the cleansing, oxygen-providing, pollution-dispersing, multitude of functions performed by the air, sea, rivers, winds, birds, animals, and plant life. All these are taken for granted, visible only as the so-called free gift of nature. It is clear that some natural resources, like forests, are renewable over time. Some, for example, minerals, are depleted through use. Some, like natural silence, are unknown to billions of people in their lifetime. Yet, noise is the most endemic and one of the most intractable of environmental problems, imposing stress, disturbing sleep, reducing efficiency, causing severe annoyance, and, in some occupations, being a major cause of deafness. Some resources are degradable through various forms of pollution or mismanagement such as land or water or the atmosphere. Others, when not in use, are instantly renewable. Because we cannot see these so clearly, we tend not to think about them as natural resources. Included in this group would be the electromagnetic spectrums that are part of the natural environment of earth and space. These make possible radio and television communications with moving vehicles on land and sea, in the air, or in outer space. This resource is not depletable, but it is rare or scarce. It is always available in infinite abundance except for that portion that is being used, and when that portion is not in use, it is instantly renewable.

While few of our resources fall into that category in terms of use, the electromagnetic spectrum demonstrates a clear characteristic of natural resources. They do not recognize national boundaries.

In any meeting between the Canadian Prime Minister and the President of the United States, the effect of acid rain on Canadian forests as a result of pollution in the United States is always a major agenda item. Sissel Roanbeck, Norway's minister for the environment, points out that Norway's pollution problem is British industry. Britain has the fourth largest emission of sulphur into the air of any country on earth. Most of it falls on Norway and the rest of Scandanavia as acid rain. French radioactive fallout from Muroroa doesn't know it belongs in Paris. When the multi-national pharmaceutical company Sandoz spills massive pollutant doses of dye and mercury into the Rhine in Switzerland, the poisons don't stop when they get to the Swiss border. The premise that the environment can be measured inside a nation-state concept (a premise embraced by Brundtland and the notion of sustainable development) is as poverty-ridden as the notion that money is the only indication of value.

The inability to attribute a market value to a part of the ecosystem does not mean that it is not worthy of consideration in the public policy equation. Yet, the treatment of the environment in the national accounts and in public policy reproduces the arrogant ideology that only money is of value, that the market is the only source of knowledge. It suggests that all of life can be condensed to this narrow and soulless view, which precipitates us, at an ever increasing pace, towards the destruction of all forms of life on the planet.

From this feminists' perspective, none of those advocating "sustainable development"—as in Lester Brown's World Watch Institute *Reports on Progress Toward a Sustainable Society*—address the indicators or suggest that "development" is any less dependent on "economic growth" than the current exploitative market. It seems to me to be just a play with words; the heart of the problem is avoided in a diligent bow to patriarchal power and its measuring rod.

The majority of the work that the majority of the people do for the majority of the time is not counted in national accounts. Without this work, no production whatsoever could proceed. The invisible work is the primary exchange in economics. These traditional economic activities and qualitative measures of the environment are more essential indicators of the state of the human condition than any other possible. A continued reliance on national account systems as the essential component in public policy planning addresses a minority of the human species and their power and privilege treats all others in a vicarious relationship to this minority.

Unless and until the activities of women and the environment assume primacy in the public policy framework, there will be no improvement in the quality of existence of the vast majority of the people of this planet. There will continue to be a pathological growth, and it might well be in the name, this time, of "sustainable development."

References

Brown, Lester. 1984 - 1990. *State of the World.* Washington, DC: Worldwatch Institute. Annual volumes on *Reports on Progress Towards a Sustainable Society.*

Galbraith, John Kenneth. 1987. *Economics in Perspective: A Critical History.* Boston: Houghton Mifflin.

Hueting, Roefle. 1983. *Use of Environmental Data in the Economic Decision-Making Process.* Contribution of the Netherlands Bureau of Statistics. U.N. Environment Program (UNEP/W.G.85/INF.11).

United Nations. 1960, 1968. *A System of National Accounts and Supporting Tables.* Statistical Office of the U.N. Studies in Methods. Series F, No. 2, Rev. 1.

Waring, Marilyn. 1988. *If Women Counted: A New Feminist Economics.* New York: Harper Collins.

Rosalie Bertell (r) talks with Marie-Thérèse Danielsson (l) in Port Vila, Vanuatu

Survival, Not Economy, Is The Bottom Line

Rosalie Bertell

In dealing with the nuclear issue, we are dealing with a case of addiction, addiction to militarism. As in most cases of addiction, those addicted to militarism are operating out of a sense of inadequacy. To use market terminology in this case, they don't have a good enough product—namely, "might makes right"—so they have to force it on others, and they have to lie to maintain their addiction. In addition, as in all cases of addiction, the addiction could not be maintained without enablers—us. The question before us now is whether our passiveness is threatening humanity's survival?

Supposedly human beings are putting up with nuclear weapons because they are giving us a sense of security. This craze-making "logic," however, puts us in the position of killing ourselves with radioactive pollution in order to survive. It also raises the serious

---

Editor's Note—Dr. Rosalie Bertell, author of *No Immediate Danger: Prognosis for a Radioactive Earth*, has testified before the Select Committee on Uranium Resources in Australian in 1980 and at the Sizewell Enquiry in Britain in 1984. A member of the Order of Grey Nuns, she now investigates the effects of low-level radiation on humans as Director of Research of the International Institute of Concern for Public Health in Toronto, Canada. She campaigns internationally against the dangers of nuclear technology.

questions of food security, reproductive security, and so on in the face of uranium mining and milling waste, nuclear emission, weapons testing fallout, and all the radioactive waste from reactors and weapons industries.

Among the effects of radioactivity on living cells, the "least worst" damage is to kill a cell entirely because with death the process ends. If a cell is merely damaged, not killed, then the damaged cell can replicate itself. If this cell happens to be a sperm or an ovum, the damage occurs in every cell of the new organism and is carried into all subsequent generations. This is reflected in an increase in still births, neonatal death, miscarriages and birth defects.

If the damaged cells are not sperm or ovum, damage at a macro level is reflected in a variety of problems: increases in cataracts, obesity, cardiovascular renal disease, impaired fertility and, of course, cancer, the latter caused by a cell's resting mechanism having been knocked out, so that it reproduces cells which also have no rest period. This rampant growth leads to cancers or non-malignant tumors.

Looking at cancer actually focuses our attention on the least of our worries. We should be looking at genetic effects and increases in immune and autoimmune diseases, disease categories which include both diabetes and AIDS, when ascertaining the effects of radiation in human populations. The International Commission on Radiological Protection (ICRP), a self-constituted committee of thirteen men, consisting of physicists from nuclear industries, radiologists and medical bureaucrats, selected tumors to focus on, not just tumor induction, but fatalities attributed to tumors. I might add parenthetically that the patterns put forward in Marilyn Waring's presentation on economic measurements hold true as well for epidemiology. Statistics for tumor fatalities only reflect deaths where cancer is the first cause of death. Many deaths are not counted as cancer induced because the cancer patient dies of pneumonia, heart attack, accident, or something else. In a population, sixty percent of the increase in cancers caused by radiation occur in people who were irradiated under the age of twenty. The damage is greater in children because irradiation that occurs during periods of rapid growth is equivalent to throwing a rock in a moving machine. Also, two-thirds of the increases occur in women who have more vulnerable tissue (especially breast and uterine). The genetic effects of natural radiation were observed by me and my colleagues on a budget of almost nothing. We did a study of the effects of natural radiation in Kerala, India. This site is often used by ICRP and the nuclear industry to play down the effects of radiation. In this meticulously done Kerala study, we matched sample populations living on the radioactive sand with similar populations not living on radioactive sand. We followed nearly 100,000 pregnancies and the following statistics emerged. In the population living in contact with the radioactive beach sand the following conditions, all genetic effects, more than doubled: Downs syndrome (four times higher) and other mental abnormalities, epilepsy, congenital deafness and blindness, cleft lip and palate, skeletal abnormalities,

Table 1. AIDS cases by age group and sex for eighteen European countries,[1] June 30, 1985

Age Group	Male	Female	Unknown	Ratio	Total	Percent
0-11 months	6	6	0	1.0	12	.98
1-4 years	6	5	0	1.2	11	.90
5-9 years	2	1	1	2.0	4	.33
10-14 years	3	0	0		3	.24
15-19 years	5	0	0		5	.41
20-29 years	207	45	0	4.6	252	20.55
30-39 years	490	28	0	17.5	518	42.25
40-49 years	295	11	0	26.8	306	24.96
50-59 years	83	8	0	10.4	91	7.42
60+ years	12	1	0	12.0	13	1.06
Unknown	11	0	0		11	.90
Totals	1120	105	1	10.7	1226	100.00

1. Austria, Belgium, Czechoslovakia, Denmark, Finalnd, France, Federal Republic of Germany, Greece, Iceland, Italy, Luxemburg, Netherlands, Norway, Poland, Spain, Sweden, Switzerland, United Kingdom.

and childless couples. These were only the conditions that were more than double those in the non-irradiated population.

The world is also facing the AIDS phenomena. This is the clincher in terms of the ICRP focusing on too little, too late! The AIDS virus is apparently an old, sophisticated retrovirus which normally affected people in their 70s, as Arsene Burny of the Department of Molecular Biology at the University of Brussels has argued. Now AIDS affects people of a much younger age, and there is a curious convergence of circumstances which explain why. If you consider the fact that people irradiated in their childhood years incur the greatest damage from radiation and if you look at the high point of atmospheric testing of nuclear weapons in the 1950s through 1963, then you would expect the distribution of AIDS sufferers to be highest among those who were children in the 1950s and early 1960s. In fact this is precisely what records of the spread of the virus show (see Table 1).

In 1985, the year for which Table 1 was compiled, those in the age group twenty to forty-nine were born between the years 1936 and 1965. Recall that the period of atmospheric nuclear testing occurred between the years 1945 and 1963. Dr. E. J. Sternglass of the University of Pittsburgh Medical School hypothesized that

> Strontium-90 and other radioisotopes in the diet during the period of atmospheric nuclear testing increased the mutation rate of the AIDS related indigenous human or animal retroviruses in bone-marrow stem cells, and also produced a cohort of susceptible individuals whose immune defenses were impaired during early development. Although A-bomb tests began in 1945, the world-wide increase in Strontium-90 in the diet did not take place until after the large H-bomb tests of the mid-50s, rising most sharply between 1962 and 1963. The greatest increase in AIDS occurred 18-19 years later when the large cohort of immune deficient infants reached maturity and were exposed to sexually transmitted diseases, causing the T-cells with the HTLV-III/LAY to multiply and the virus to spread wherever conditions favored high rates of sexual contact or other efficient means of transmission

directly to the bloodstream. . . . Damage to the immune system is supported by rises in pneumonia, influenza and other infections among newborn during the height of nuclear weapons testing, as well as by animal studies showing clearly detectable decreases in bone-marrow cellularity at Strontium-90 exposures in the 10-100 millirad range.[2]

What is even worse than the table above shows is the fact that the fallout from atmospheric nuclear tests circulated two and a half times around the globe and concentrated in the tropics, northern temperate zones and in the Arctic regions. Central Africa had extraordinarily high levels of nuclear fallout contamination due to the Christmas Island nuclear tests. The conclusion that the massive outbreak of an AIDS epidemic is the result of damaged immune systems should come as no surprise. The AIDS epicenter, to use a seismological term, in central Africa should also come as no surprise. The AIDS area in Africa is also the former Belgian Congo—center for uranium mining and resting place of the radioactive uranium waste. The nuclear fall-out of 1962-1963 may have been a "last straw."

To summarize, the facts which we need to consider are the following:

1. The retrovirus which has been identified as causing AIDS is well developed from an evolutionary point of view. It is not a new mutation, but one which has evolved over many years. It used to affect those over 70 years of age.

2. The implication of fact (1) is that there has been a change in the ability of young adults to cope with and overcome this retrovirus since it affects most significantly people between the ages of 20 and 45 years old.

3. Facts (1) and (2) imply a damaged immune system before exposure to the AIDS virus.

---

2. E. J. Sternglass, "In-Utero Exposure of Bone Marrow Cells to Strontium-90 as a Possible Co-Factor in the Etiology of AIDS," paper presented at AAAS Annual Meeting, Philadephia, PA, May 29, 1986: paper nuber 810, session 8A.

4. In the U.S. (and perhaps elsewhere) the AIDS generation (cohort) is also afflicted with unusually high rates of neonatal and infant mortality during their birth years, childhood cancers and young adult affliction with deaths from toxic shock syndrome, chronic fatigue (Epstein-Barr virus), higher cancer incidence rates. This generation also dropped out of school at an unusually high rate and turned to drugs. In other words, this is obviously a damaged generation.

5. The major damaging agent between 1945 and 1963 was nuclear fallout by atmospheric nuclear testing. Those born between 1945 and 1963 are now between ages 28 and 45 years; in 1980 they were between ages 18 and 35 years. This is the AIDS generation).

6. There was heavy fallout in the U.S. (due to Pacific and Nevada testing 1946-1963) and in Africa (due to hydrogen bomb testing in Christmas Islands in 1962-1963). The AIDS epidemic began in these areas. The affected area of Africa includes the former Belgian Congo, site of uranium mining and tailings waste, active prior to World War II.

7. There is mounting evidence that nuclear radiation damages the blood monocytes, the white blood cells which turn on the lymphocytes, the blood cellular immune system which in turn is designed to destroy bacteria, viruses, and tumors. AIDS also attacks the monocytes first before overwhelming the lymphocyte immune system.

Therefore: We call for full investigation and disclosure of the causes of AIDS worldwide with a new line of research including nuclear contamination as a predisposing cause.

We call for an end to all nuclear pollution (uranium, nuclear industries and nuclear related weapons) world wide.

We call for recognition of immune strengthening medicines, such as calf thymus therapy, as a preventive strategy. While transmissions of the virus is important for spreading AIDS among the immune damaged (or fetus/embryo), prevention of immune damage should be the primary medical response to halt the spread of AIDS.

Two other points I would like to make are first that there is more protection in international law for soldiers than civilians. A good strategy would be to bring the case for atomic veterans to the Human

Rights Court. Second, a possible way to handle nuclear waste in a responsible fashion is to demand Monitored Retrievable Storage (MRS). We can only build containers that last thirty or so years; therefore, we have to set up a constant repackaging program.

Actions To be Taken

Over the next twelve month period, each delegate or group of delegates should go to their own countries and educate themselves on the International Commission on Radiological Protection and the lack of:

- Women's participation
- Epidemiologists' participation.
- Doctors' participation (occupational and public health medicine, oncology, medical genetics),
- Biologists' participation.

Question both its structure and authority. Try to change the focus of concern to include genetic effects, immune and autoimmune system deficiencies, cardiovascular/renal system effects, etc. Counting cancer fatalities has deflected concern away from genetic problems and other radiation damage. Additionally, as recently admitted by ICRP, their estimate of cancer deaths per unit of radiation has been too low for the past thirty years. These thirteen men's recommendations were opposed by 800 scientists in a written petition in 1988. They need to be relieved of their self-appointed task of recommending radiation standards.

Top — Working committee: (l - r) Ann Symonds, Marilyn Waring, Mavis Robertson, and Marie-Thérèse Danielsson. *Bottom* — (l - r) Mavis Robertson, Lenora Foerstel, and Kuini Bavadra who leads the coalition of the Fijian Labour Party and the National Federation Party in opposing the U.S. backed dictatorship and its attempt to re-write Fiji's constitution.

Colonization In French Polynesia

Marie-Thérèse Danielsson

The Europeans who during the past two hundred years gradually have invaded and taken control of the Pacific islands have all been extremely ethnocentric. Or in other words, they were convinced that their own civilization was the highest and best in the world and that all changes they introduced were highly beneficial to the poor savages, as they used to call the natives. Those who most firmly held this belief were, of course, the missionaries, who firmly maintained that to be a good Christian a native must also dress, live, and work in the European manner. This ethnocentric outlook has also dominated the policies imposed by European countries, which during the last century established colonies in the Pacific, for the aim of all British, German, and French governors has everywhere been to introduce a European

Editor's Note—Marie-Thérèse Danielsson has spent most of her life as a resident of French Polynesia. She is active in local politics, women's organization, and in the nuclear-free movement. With her husband, Bengt Danielsson, she has carried out anthropological research in the Pacific and has witnessed the results of French colonization of the Polynesian people. The Danielssons have written numerous books, including a six volume history of French Polynesia, *Le Mémorial Polynésian* (1976-1980). Their most recent book, *Poisoned Reign*, condemns French nuclear colonialism in the Pacific.

type of political system and economy. The result has always been disastrous for the islanders, even in the few instances when they accepted the policies of their colonial masters and themselves voluntarily contributed to the changes.

Not surprisingly, the most horrifying example of this non-religious form of missionary work can today be found in Tahiti, the main island in French Polynesia, which together with New Caledonia, Wallis, and Futuna are the last old-fashioned colonies on earth. Although Tahiti became a French protectorate in 1842 and a colony in 1880, it attracted until recently extremely few French settlers, simply because the island was so remote from the "mother country" and, even worse, totally devoid of exploitable natural resources. A tragic turning point was reached, however, in 1963, when France began in earnest to colonize Tahiti and the surrounding islands such as Austral, Taumotu, and Marquesas Islands which make up French Polynesia. In contrast, Great Britain, in conformity with the U.N. resolution 1514, launched her Pacific colonies on the road which within a few years led to independence. The reason for this retrograde French policy was General Charles de Gaulle's megalomaniac ambition to endow France with nuclear weapons, which had already manifested itself by a series of tests in the Sahara desert. By then, the Soviet Union and the U.S.A. had agreed to make all future testing underground. But with a total disregard for the health hazards to which he exposed whole nations of innocent people, General de Gaulle decided nevertheless to use henceforth the two atolls, Moruroa and Fangataufa, in French Polynesia for exploding his atomic bombs in the atmosphere.

The radioactive pollution from the forty-four atmospheric and one hundred-twenty-three underground tests which have been made since then has resulted in countless cancer diseases, miscarriages, birth defects, and psychological disturbances. On top of this, the stationing of tens of thousands of soldiers, including a huge number of foreign legionnaires, has caused tremendous social problems. But even worse in the long run has been the annual arrival of more than one thousand civilian Frenchmen who practically all have settled in Tahiti where they have easily made a living and often a fortune by selling goods and services to the French troops and colonial officials or directly to the army and administration. With their families they number today about 30,000 and they totally dominate the economy. Many of the 10,000 descendants of the Chinese coolies, who were imported in the 1860s to work on cotton and sugar plantations in Tahiti, are also sufficiently clever businessmen who benefit greatly from the economic boom. This is also the case of a few thousand Demis or Mestizoes while the Tahitians who number 70,000 are utterly unable to compete in business with these other ethnic groups. The only thing they can hope for is actually some low-paid, menial work, but even these opportunities are few.

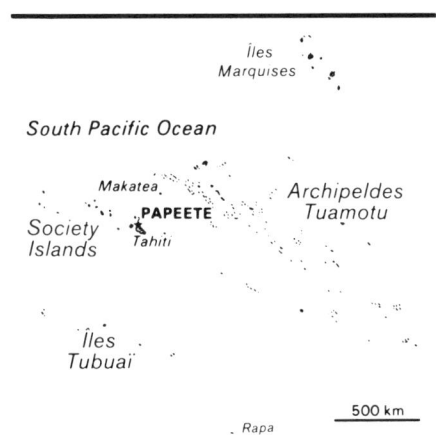

French Polynesia
Overseas territory of France. Population, 190,181: 78% Polynesian, 12% Chinese, 6% local French, 4% non-resident French. Total area, 3,942 km². Major industries: subsistence farming, tourism, and military.

Before 1963 all Tahitian families owned enough land to grow all the food they needed and to make saleable copra from their coconut palms. But French businessmen and commercial companies have during the past decades managed to acquire—often with dishonest methods—much of their land, which has also become scarce due to the high birth rate among the Tahitians. The steady increase of young Tahitian men and women without land and without work has created an explosive social situation, which first erupted in October 1987. Riots broke out in the capital, Papeete, during which fifty shops were looted and burnt down. The authorities have tried to create jobs for these poverty-stricken proletarians by developing tourism. But in spite of the huge sums spent on promotion in Europe, America, and Japan, the annual number of tourists visiting French Polynesia during the past ten years has increased only from 100,000 to 140,000 and the hotels are rarely more than half-filled. The reason is, of course, that foreign visitors do not any longer find what has motivated them to make the expensive trip—the idyllic South Sea paradise that Tahiti used in the days of Captain Cook. Since the Tourist Board continues to propagate this false image, visitors are terribly shocked, when they step off their airplane or cruise ship and suddenly find themselves entangled in heavy automobile traffic and see along the road only modern houses inhabited by well-dressed Europeans and some natives.

If they dare to walk along some trails winding into small valleys, along the rivers, they are shocked by the poverty and the promiscuity of certain slums, where the natives from other islands live, after having been attracted to the main island by the promise of jobs.

Despite many meetings in Paris and in Tahiti discussions around so-called round tables, official visits—the last one by the president of the Republic himself—and many more promises, the pressure and the influence of colonialism have never been as strong and more difficult to stop. They work in many different forms and in many dubious ways. The youngest children start in classes of twenty-five to thirty with a school teacher who speaks French. Tahitian is used only for songs and only if the teacher is fluent in it. Many children who live in Polynesian speaking families are in that way prevented from participating in their own culture. During the following years, French books and French curriculum are used, even in the study of history, geography and natural sciences. A university has been established, on the French model and is supposed to spread the French culture in the whole Pacific.

Of course, the most important means of indoctrination is through the media. Ninety-five percent of TV and radio programs come from France and are in French. The only news from the rest of the Pacific comes from a single French reporter situated in Australia, who covers the whole English speaking Pacific region from Sydney. There is no educational program for adults which could be so valuable in such a vast territory, where radio is often the only link with the outside world.

There are two newspapers in French Polynesia. They belong to the same owner, the French news magnate, Mr. Hersant. The journalists are mostly French and very few have lived in the islands for a long time. Thus, they ignore the most elementary facts about the people's history, customs, and culture of the country. Finally, the representative of Agence France Press (AFP) is a high-ranking civil servant, working in the High-Commissioner's office, as Press Officer.

All these aspects of colonization are not really new. They are only emphasized by the increasing French influence on the life of the Polynesian people.

Top – "Bravo," photo by Defense Nuclear Agency. *Bottom* – Ellen Boas lived on Rongelap in 1954 when "Bravo" was exploded on Bikini Atoll. Note the scars on her neck from two operations for thyroid cancer, a late effect of the radioactive fallout. The child is her grandson (Photo by Gary Kildea).

Nuclear Colonialism In The Pacific

Glenn Alcalay

Having spent the past year conducting research among the women of the Marshall Islands (in Micronesia) has made me reflect even more profoundly upon the brutal impact on women in the Pacific from the twin evils of colonialism and militarism. It was here in the Marshalls that the United States—immediately following the militarily unnecessary and experimental atomic bombings at Hiroshima and Nagasaki—proceeded to wage undeclared nuclear war on the people of the Marshall Islands in the remote reaches of the western Pacific. Decades after the last hydrogen bomb was exploded here, the Marshallese are still struggling to untangle the panoply of radiation effects—both to the health of the people and the environment—from the nuclear tests.

On March 1, 1954, the U.S. unleashed its largest and dirtiest H-bomb (code named "Bravo") at Bikini Atoll, a bomb *1,200 times* the size of the relatively tiny Hiroshima atomic bomb. Designed by

---

Editor's note—Glenn Alcalay is a Ph.D. candidate in medical anthropology at the New School for Social Research in New York City. He has been active for the rights of Pacific peoples for the past sixteen years since he was a Peace Corp volunteer in the Marshall Islands. Alcalay also heads the National Committee for Radiation Victims (95 Cabrini Blvd. #3-0, New York, NY 10033).

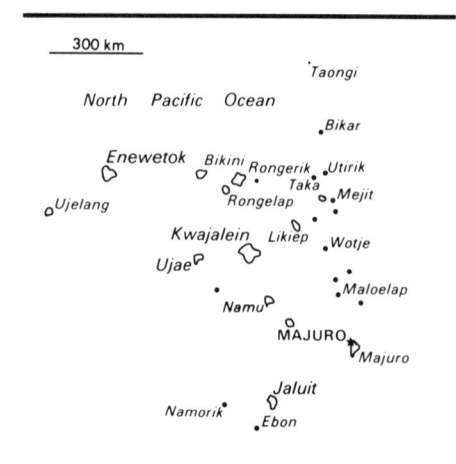

Marshall Islands
Independent from United States in 1986 but U.S. controlled under the Compact of Free Association. Population, 43,417: Micronesian. Total area, 181 km².

Edward Teller, "Bravo" was intended to produce maximum radioactive fallout (utilizing the "Ulam" design). Before the explosion, the Atomic Energy Commission established an international network of radiological monitoring stations to trace the worldwide fallout patterns.

Although the U.S. cited unexpected "wind shifts" for the "accidental" contamination of numerous inhabited atolls downwind of Bikini, the factual record suggests a more sinister explanation for the widespread nuclear contamination of populated islands. According to the senior Air Force weatherperson, Gene Curbow, stationed one hundred-thirty-five miles to the east of Bikini, the fallout from "Bravo" was not unexpected. In a 1982, *New York Times* interview, Curbow explained that "For weeks prior to 'Bravo' the winds were heading from Bikini to Rongerik, and never 'shifted' as the U.S. contends." When asked why it took nearly three decades to reveal this important information, Curbow replied that "It was a mixture of patriotism and ignorance, I guess."

Moreover, a recently released Pentagon document added more fuel to the "Bravo" controversy. In a 1982 Defense Nuclear Agency report it was stated that "The midnight weather briefing (i.e., a mere six hours before 'Bravo' exploded) indicated that winds at 20,000 feet were heading for [inhabited] Rongelap to the east." That the commander of the Joint Task Force did not cancel the "Bravo" test with such an alarming weather forecast leads one to conclude that the Marshallese downwind of Bikini *were in fact part of the experiment.*

As one of the "experimentees," Mwendrik Kebenli of Rongelap recounted to me some years ago the following narrative about her personal encounter with the thermonuclear age:

> I was on Rongelap in 1954. I awoke very early in the morning and saw the flash of light in the western sky and did not know what it was. The sky turned red and I was very surprised; everyone was really scared. Later when the powder fell on my island, children cried and complained that it was hurting them and that it felt quite hot on their skin. They tried to wash it off but it did not relieve the pain. The powder was yellow and like flour, and it made us lose our appetites.

Following the evacuation days later of the Rongelap community (100 miles east of Bikini) and the people of Utirik (270 miles from Bikini) to Kwajalein, the acute symptoms of radiation sickness were playing havoc with the irradiated Marshallese. Feeling bewildered and disoriented by their sudden arrival at a military base, the Marshallese suffered beta burns, depressed blood counts, the loss of bodily hair, and the uncertainty associated with the unknown problems that may erupt in the future.

Mwendrik recalls that the early period after their exposure was just the mere foreshadowing of what lay ahead,

> When we returned to Rongelap (in 1957) our life was very different; we still had many new problems with our health, and these are still occurring. Many women gave birth to things [which looked] like an octopus, and some babies were born without bones in parts of their bodies.

Between 1946 and 1958, the U.S. exploded sixty-six atomic and hydrogen bombs at Bikini and Enewetok in the Marshalls: several H-bombs in the megaton range scattered radioactive ash down upon numerous inhabited atolls. The atoll communities of Bikini and Enewetok, having been displaced for the nuclear tests, remain societies in exile, being referred to as the "nuclear nomads."

Following the acute initial effects of radiation disease, the late effects of exposure began to appear in 1963 (nine years after "Bravo") in the form of thyroid abnormalities. Thirty-seven years after their exposure, the Marshallese have contracted hundreds of thyroid disorders, and numerous other radiation related diseases which are believed to be the result of radiation.

Because of their ongoing fears and uncertainties about living in a radioactive environment, the people of Rongelap decided to abandon their home atoll. In May 1985, with the assistance of the Greenpeace ship "Rainbow Warrior" the Rongelapese moved to a tiny and inhospitable island called Mejato within the Kwajalein Atoll. It was during this Greenpeace campaign when the "Rainbow Warrior" was scheduled to protest ongoing French nuclear testing near Tahiti that agents from France's DSGE (the French equivalent of the American CIA) sabotaged the environmental group's ship in New Zealand, killing one crew member.

As the newest member of the "nuclear nomads" society, the Rongelap people have become the latest casualties of the nuclear testing legacy: living temporarily on a "borrowed" island, the Rongelapese are awaiting the outcome of independent radiological survey of their home atoll to determine if they may safely return.

Having been hit with high levels of radioactive fallout, suffering the short and long-term consequences of latent radiation diseases and the consequences of sociological dislocation, some of the atoll communities affected by the fallout have now become divided over the settlement money (a tiny fraction of the net damages) given by the U.S. government in a hotly contested political settlement in 1983. Needless to say, the legacy of the nuclear tests has virtually destroyed the lives of thousands of Marshall Islanders. One of the long-term questions stemming from the nuclear tests concerns the possibility of radiation induced damage to human reproduction, known clinically as congenital anomalies.[1] Despite flat denials of these problems by

---

1. I am conducting a massive study of these problems by comparing women's reproductive histories from atoll communities closest to the former nuclear test sites with women who reside farthest away to determine the extent of these problems and a demographic map of their occurrance. The findings of my study will be available in the Fall of 1991.

the U.S. government, Marshallese women continue to complain of an increased number of miscarriages, stillbirths, and children born with birth defects from the nuclear tests.

Another major consequence of U.S. militarism in the Marshall Islands concerns the socio-cultural destruction associated with the Pentagon's strategic missile laboratory at Kwajalein Atoll. Serving as a "catcher's mitt" for incoming ballistic missiles from California's Vandenberg Air Force Base (as well as missiles launched from ocean-going submarines), Kwajalein has become a key site for the testing of important components of the SDI or "star wars" program.

Having taken prime islands in the Kwajalein complex for military purposes, the indigenous Marshallese have been forced to live on a miniscule and unforgiving island, Ebeye, known throughout the region as the "slum of the Pacific." Comprising a mere one-tenth of a square mile, Ebeye has become a blighted urban center (the second largest after Majuro, the capital) which is the home to some 10,000 Marshallese, making it perhaps *the* most densely populated place in the world!

While 3,000 American contract workers (and some military personnel) associated with the "Star Wars" program live and work in a manicured country-club-like setting on a three-square mile island, the impoverished Marshallese exist in horrendous squalor just three miles away in what some refer to as a biological time-bomb waiting to explode. While some 900 Marshallese fill the least desirable jobs (mostly as janitors and housemaids) and serve as a pool of cheap labor, the situation at Kwajalein and Ebeye closely resembles the apartheid arrangement in South Africa, replete with the contrast between Pretoria's hillside manors juxtaposed with the bantustan "homelands."

Cramped onto the inhospitable island of Ebeye, a range of diseases plague the urbanized Marshallese, including the world's highest prevalence rate of adult-onset (Type II) diabetes—triggered by a radical shift toward a western diet—as well as malnutrition, hypertension, stroke, and other preventable diseases. Added to this unhealthy brew are the usual maladaptive features linked to rapid westernization and poverty—youth gang warfare, crime, and other forms of violence.

According to Dr. Neal Palofax, a physician with the U.S. Public Health Service based in Majuro, the Marshalls boast the dubious distinction of having one the highest suicide rates in the world. During a three-month period between October and December 1990, there were six suicide deaths by young men on Ebeye (a seventh attempt failed when the rope around his neck broke). Out of a feeling of sheer desperation, five hundred-thirty Ebeye mothers wrote a letter to President Amata Kabua requesting that the government set the legal drinking age back up to 21-years of age instead of the recently lowered legal age of 18-years. On the surface—and because most the the suicides were alcohol related—this cry of help by the Ebeye women seemed to be a rational response to an ongoing socio-cultural epidemic afflicting young males between the ages of sixteen and twenty-six.

Unfortunately, raising the drinking age in the Marshalls will do little to stem the tide of young Marshallese men destroying themselves in unprecedented numbers. After all, young men from around the Pacific likewise drink to excess—as in Fiji or in Tonga—yet it is only in the Marshalls (and also in Chuuk, formerly Truk, likewise administered by the United States) where young men feel the necessity for killing themselves in record numbers. Alcohol merely lessens the inhibition to do something (like destroy oneself) that one already deeply desires; it is an effect of the desperation people feel in the Marshalls, not its cause.

What then are some of the *causes* of this horrific desperation? Following nearly a century of intensive colonialism by the Japanese and Americans, the vulnerable Marshallese have become *de facto* second-class citizens in their own nation. Having been ruled by racist colonial administrators who continually belittled and denigrated Marshallese culture and social practices, the Marshallese were no match for the powerful foreign militarists and insensitive bureaucrats who dictate policies that helped to undermine and erode traditional Marshallese society.

Aside from the direct effects of post-War U.S. nuclear and strategic missile exercises, the intentional creation of economic dependency following the recommendations contained in the infamous 1963 "Soloman Report" has set up an artificial economy based on annual cash infusions from the U.S. Treasury which amounts to some 90% of the Marshallese budget. As one walks through the back alleys of Majuro or Ebeye, one sees groups of young unemployed males idly hanging around with little to do. One is overwhelmed by the sense of despair these young men must feel in a post-colonial society where most avenues of existence lead only to a dead-end. Alcohol consumption merely serves as the intoxicating catalyst for suicide; a century of erosion of Marshallese cultural integrity, dignity, and feelings of self-worth during harsh colonial practices has severely damaged the identity of young Marshallese (and Chuukese) males, with suicide being the escape-valve from an otherwise existential nightmare amidst a former tropical paradise.

In the Marshallese milieu, it is the women here who are literally holding the society together. A graphic index of this reality is the fact that the male to female suicide rate is about twenty-five to one! In a matrilineal society—where land (the most important commodity in the land-starved Marshall Islands) is reckoned through the female line—it is the women who maintain their historic pride and feelings of self-worth amidst the rubble of the crisis afflicting male identity. In my own travels around the outer islands, it seems quite obvious to me that women continue to embody the collective spirit that is the foundation of Marshallese culture, a culture that dates back about 4,000 years before the present era.

In contrast, men have not fared so successfully during the massive upheavals associated with a century of colonialism. For the majority of Marshallese men who are losing in the struggle to adapt to a cash economy—an effect of the asymmetrical and artificial economy imposed by the U.S.—the attendant loss of cultural pride and feelings of self-worth go hand in hand with the perception of not being a successful breadwinner in an increasingly monetary economy. With copra prices at an all-time low for outer islanders and with massive and structural unemployment in urban centers, the traditional role of males in Marshallese society has been seriously undermined. Evidence of this, aside from the aforementioned suicide epidemic, is manifest in a spiralling upsurge of familial violence, including wife-beating. This unfortunate syndrome is only now getting the attention it deserves.

Another facet of the problems facing men here concerns the extremely high birth rate among the Marshallese. With an average of 8.2 children for each Marshallese female—one of the world's highest birth rates—it is the Marshallese men who are responsible for wishing to keep their women "barefoot and pregnant," thus controlling the fertility of women. Most women I have spoken with explain that the change of traditional to western society—and the concomitant high costs of supporting new western life-styles—has made them opt for smaller families. It is the men, these women tell me, who insist on having lots of babies, and I have even heard of some men beating their wives when they discovered them taking birth control pills. Fortunately, the Norplant form of birth control is catching on here (more than 1,000 women out of a present Marshallese population of some 47,000 are currently using this method) to help bring the birth rate down.

Although women are proving to be the backbone of contemporary society, there still is a lot of educational and organizational work to be done in the Marshall Islands. I recently spoke with a Papua New Guinea women from her country's Department of Home Affairs and Youth about the situation of women in the Marshalls. During her recent visit here—following similar visits to Vanuatu and the Cook Islands—my Papua New Guinea friend explained that the women of the Marshalls seemed further behind their sisters in the other Pacific nations she visited. Attributing this problem to a lack of information and extreme isolation, my friend reasoned that Marshallese women—despite being traditionally in control of land—conspicuously lacked the political sophistication and knowledge about other international struggles affecting women which would be useful for understanding the domestic difficulties afflicting women here. My Papua New Guinea friend, when queried about a possible solution for the women here replied, "What the women of the Marshals need is nothing short of a revolution."

The Vanuatu Congress—of which this anthology is a part—reminds us more than ever that more networking and solidarity building are needed across regional and national boundaries. Whether they be Palestinian women involved in the Intifada, Irish women engaged in the struggle for sovereignty in Belfast, British women working for disarmament at Greenham Common, the courageous women of GABRIELA working for women's rights in the Philippines, or the brave women of Belau fighting to maintain that country's unprecedented anti-nuclear constitution—greater coordination and networking is called for in our struggle on behalf of women. In this respect, let us not forget our Pacific Island sisters here in the Marshall Islands.

photo by Glenn Alcalay
This aerial photo of Ebeye, Kwajalein Atoll, shows the dense crowding of 10,000 people on a mere one-tenth of a square mile. These people serve as a supply of cheap labor for the U.S. "Star Wars" missile complex at Kwajalein, just three miles away.

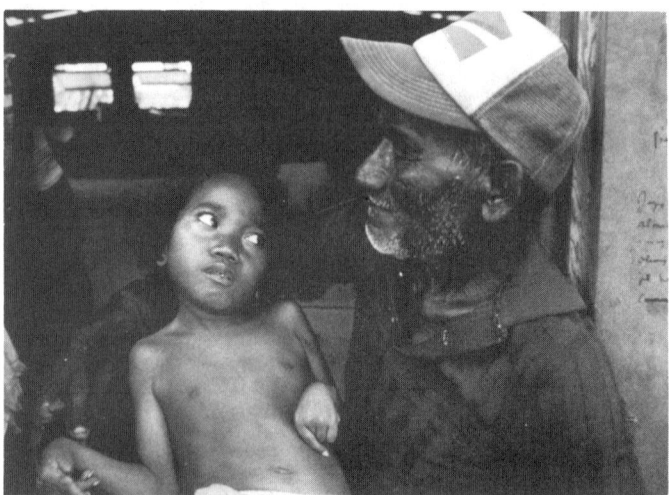

Top — A street scene on Ebeye, well-known as the "slum of the Pacific" (photo by Glenn Alcalay). *Bottom* — A young Rongelap girl with serious birth defects. This photo was taken in May 1985 by Fernando Pereira, the Greenpeace photographer killed aboard the "Rainbow Warrior" when it was bombed by French agents in New Zealand.

Nuclear Neo-Colonialism In The Ocean Of Peace

**Leslie W. Scott
Diana B. Sheridan**

We arrived in the South Pacific with a perspective colored by conflicting images as diverse as the island cultures themselves. Rooted in our imperialist upbringing, one procreative image invoked an idyllic paradise represented by Gauguin's lush Tahiti with its ripe young women offering fruits in welcoming gestures to their colonizers. Another contrasting image conjured a nightmare of annihilation epitomized by a nuclear "hot" and devastated Rongelap laid waste by some 215 nuclear test explosions in the South Pacific conducted between 1945 and 1984. Framing both these vivid images was our own experience as activists and academicians in critiquing our nation's—the United States'—imperialist reliance on women's continued invisibility and oppression.

We left the South Pacific with profound insight and commitment grounded in contextualized images of vital, diverse women struggling to restore to their "Ocean of Peace," a viable ecology, a harmonious social climate, and a sustainable economic livelihood. Bringing to the International Pacific Policy Congress an abstract understanding of the relationship between Pacific Island women and their security concerns engendered a compelling need to concretize connections between the immediacy of their nuclearized world and our own. Our shared ocean as well as our shared experiences taught us that a politics of resistance and the policy questions that such a politics comprehends demand diverse yet frequently parallel forms of opposition.

As women devising methods of opposition, we experience in militarization as well as industrialization a social process that inevitably results in the production of violence which brutalizes women and many men everywhere. We observe that socially constructed sexist relationships and gender hierarchies on which militarized society erects itself stretches across the planet and into the farthest reaches. Regardless of the cultural context or stage of industrial development, each State relies on its particular form of masculine privilege in conjunction with class and race inequities to shape a politics of control. Defined as national security policy, this militarized peace is the means through which patriarchal capitalism has smashed the security of our community as women—whether in the Pacific Island nations or in the industrialized nations of the North—by inventing property ownership, the nuclear family, and a transcendent Westernized male deity.

For each of us engaged in resisting this policy of military security based on the constant exploitation of all life, we first must expose it as a system of mystified patriarchal control institutionalized in an elite State. At the Congress, the open exchange of ideas with Pacific women engaged in active resistance provided us with new insights that we have integrated into our own methods of resistance at home in the United States. We now envision our priorities to be two-fold: first, to uncover the myths that underpin this armed system of threat, and second, to argue for authentic security that derives primarily from the reasonable expectation of well-being. As feminists and women activists devoted to fulfilling expectations of well-being, we discern in the relevance of women's experience a new multi-dimensional approach to security that is both value explicit and based largely on the interpretation of relationships within and between the diverse communities.

In assessing these myths of patriarchy, we find that the principal security myth incorporates a rationale that justifies the existence of States based on the assumed need of women, children, and elders for protection. Women at the Congress noted that intervention has always been more difficult to justify when there are no female or child victims to flaunt before the public. At the very moment of our Congress, George Bush was eagerly citing Amnesty International's report on the alleged killings by Iraqi soldiers of babies in Kuwaiti hospitals as another essential reason why the United States should use the full force of its national security appratus to resolve what was nothing more than a minor border dispute between Iraq and Kuwait.[1] The second myth explains that some States and their citizens are ordained as the "chosen," as more equal than others to carry out this "protection." A subtext of this myth, repeatedly pointed out to us, is that women of the United States are equal and liberated while women in other parts of the world are not. The striking image of United States military women tank drivers in the Persian Gulf contrasted with veiled Saudi women unable to obtain a driver's license resonates with that of the bikini-clad women tourists free to stroll the beaches of Vanuatu in contrast to their hotel cleaning women who are required to keep their shoulders and knees covered.

The third myth, originating in the aftermath of World War II, relies on an underlying assumption that development security is intended to liberate women, children, and other disenfranchised groups from their "underdeveloped" lives. In partnership with multi-national corporations, development has served as the contemporary, ideological agent of genocide as well as a linchpin of the national security policies of the United States, France, and Great Britain. Evidence that this myth has actually proven to be a mechanism for controlling economies and cultures was raised frequently in the dialogues conducted at the Congress. For example, the struggle of the Kanaks in French-controlled New Caledonia illustrates how the devastating consequences of this myth have been played out[2]. The life-styles of the industrialized North

---

1. Since the war, Amnesty International has withdrawn its report and the charges of killing babies and rape have been proven false. This has, of course, not changed the practice of myth-purveyors in the least way—*editor*.

2. See Susanna Ounei, "The Plight of the Kanak People in New Caledonia" on pages 57-62 above—*editor*.

depend on "developing" the lives of the peoples of the South into enslaved consumers or resources from which wealth can be extracted.

These myths, while serving to prop up the US national security posture in the world, have produced not only insecurity rather than security but have enabled a type of neo-colonialism that is both ecocidal and ethnicidal. As evidenced at the Bikini Atoll, Bhopal, and Chernobyl—to name but a few of the most egregious examples—ecocide is the destruction of ecological viability and possibility. Ethnicide, or the annihilation of cultural groups, is often for First Nation peoples or indigenous peoples of the land inseparable from either ecocide or genocide. The egregious examples here are, of course, Native Americans and Aboriginal Australians.

The interrelationship of these phenomena are poignantly evidenced on Johnston Atoll, a tiny coral reef in the central Pacific held as an unincorporated territory of the United States. The women of the Congress placed Johnston Atoll at the epicenter of the ever expanding assault on the entire Pacific environment, including the ocean, the land, the atmosphere, and the people. The atoll serves as a microcosm of a complex human problem since its appropriation by the United States as a disposal site for toxic substances that should never have been produced in the first place.

Since 1971, this atoll has become the dumping ground for deadly chemicals such as agent orange, mustard gas, the nerve agents VX and GB. Most recently, the enormous US chemical weapons stockpile located in West Germany has been

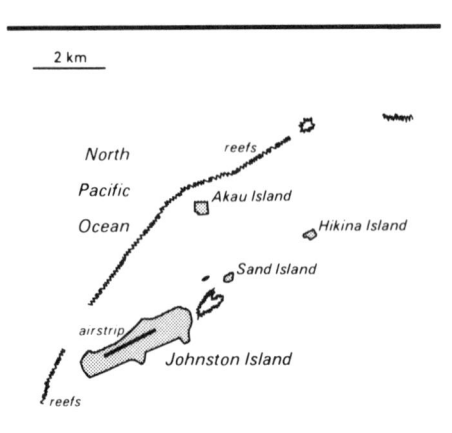

Johnston Atoll
Unincorporated territory of the United States, administered by U.S. Defense Nuclear Agency. Population, 1,203 all U.S. government personnel and contractors. Total area, 2.8 km^2.

transported to Johnston Island. Weapons production, testing, and disposal are conducted in the name of national security—without, however, assuming responsibility for the lands and peoples affected. This nuclear neo-colonialism is done in the name of economic development, touting an increase in jobs, skills acquisition, and increased consumerism. Not mentioned, of course, is the expense to the people's culture, history, and future. The real issue is not which scientist, development specialist, or military strategist is correct regarding the technological aspects of this debate, but whether the integrity of Pacific peoples is respected, enabling them to describe and define their own fate. As Poka Laenui of the World Council of Indigenous Peoples states, "Pacific Islanders protesting the transfer of these stockpiles are asking, 'Who are you to sit in judgment over the fate of our lives? Who are you to decide when or when not to risk our environment?'"

In addition to the parallels emerging from these gender-based myths of security, we recognize other useful parallels between our world and those of our sisters in the Pacific. These parallels focus on the ethnicidal and ecocidal exercises of power that States project in what is often rationalized as a national security situation. Two comparisons became immediately obvious and significant in the Congress and worthy as well of further research and action for us both.

The relationships between politics and ethnicity are very complex. Right-wing elites, whether governmental or trans-national, often benefit from and so promote the preservation of local ethnic groups while opposing any sort of pan-ethnic unity. Subsistence communities and plantations, as well as the factories of trans-national corporations, often co-exist in a lopsided dependence on local, colonized labor that can be easily converted into empire building armies by their militarized colonial masters.

Yet the political Left, while recognizing intellectually the value of preserving diverse cultural groups, has often understood ethnicity as social class. In this analysis, the Left has attempted to assimilate the "disenfranchised" into the claustrophobic, homogenizing identity of the State or Movement, catalyzing destructive and competing struggles for autonomy and political pluralism. Such forced integration, often including relocation/migration, can annihilate cultural and ecological viability as readily as Right-wing segregationism.

The parallel here is one between Fiji and Oregon in the context of a politics of neo-colonialist economic restructuring. Fiji has a complex colonial history, yet one propped up by a typical British system of indentured labor; in this instance "imported" from India. This arrangement served the British very well. The indigenous groups, unwilling to become landless laborers, were allowed to retain their cultural autonomy, while Indians, who were known quantities to the British, became a new social class that although landless, soon dominated commerce in the imposed, colonial economy. For nearly 100 years, two groups of differently disenfranchised—landless Indo-Fijians and economically disempowered native tribal peoples—struggled for political influence. In 1987, the newly elected Coalition Party, that had come very close to creating an assimilationist politics of national unity, was overthrown in a military coup led by tribal chiefs and backed by the United States. Its proposed Constitution is explicitly racist and totalitarian, yet it is being promoted in the name of the preservation of tribal/cultural autonomy.

Many of us in Oregon have long felt colonized economically and politically by the timber industry and its various governmental agents, both state and national. It has been in the name of both economic growth and security that we have been told to stand aside while Oregon's wildly beautiful and diverse ecological communities have been ravaged. Simultaneously, its 100 year old indentured labor community was being reduced and replaced by a combination of non-sustainable harvesting practices, raw log exports, and mechanized labor-saving, industrial technology. Disingenuous timber barons and their obsequious government hacks have developed an extremely effective double-speak, preaching integrationist, highly compromised environmental management "solutions" to the liberals while telling logging families that their disappearing livelihoods and communities are due to human-hating, owl-loving environmentalists. In both Oregon and Fiji, authentic security, defined as social and ecological well-being, is the victim of a politics that destroys the common ground of concern.

A second and more obvious parallel is that of the Hanford Nuclear Reservation with Johnston Atoll. Hanford is a 560 square mile island carved out of south-central Washington in the 1940s as part of the Manhattan Project; its task was to create the nuclear material (plutonium) for the bomb eventually dropped on Nagasaki. In the process, several thousand people, predominantly Native American people, were forcibly relocated; either "compensated" financially for the confiscation of their land or moved onto newly delineated peripheral reservations. The entire project was shrouded in a cloak of national security secrecy so dense that it is only in the last decade beginning to be stripped away. For all these years, the most vile and virulent waste products that militarized masculinity has been able to invent have been dumped onto and into the "god-awful desert" without a thought of the consequences for any life, present or future.

Today, faced with an unprecedented disposal dilemma at over two hundred different sites, the United States government is again, in the name of national security, moving to consolidate the problem in two or three of the country's most hospitable communities (those in which exhortations to jobs and patriotism are most easily deployed). Disguised in the ingratiating, equivocal language of "new, safe technology," the U.S. Department of Energy is moving quickly to obscure the disposal problem in order to revitalize the nuclear weapons/power complex.

Over 100,000 people living downwind from Hanford have been exposed to more radioactivity than were the Japanese in World War II; many thousands have died. This statement is not meant to diminish in any way the horror of that unconscionable act of war. The point we insist on making, however, is that our government has not declared war on the people of Washington, Oregon, and Idaho; in fact, all of this is being done in the name of protecting those people, of saving their lives, of making them secure! Indeed, every person on the planet is said to have some plutonium in her or him; every centimeter of the earth is contaminated by some form of toxic fallout. Yet, we still lack the technology to specify the nature or to identify the presence of all that we have spewed into the water and air and tissue of living things. How can we possibly declare such ecocidal and nest-fouling waste safe to incinerate, whether on Johnston Atoll or in Richland, Washington? How can we ignore the ethnicidal consequences of forced relocation and the extinction of the salmon for peoples whose lives are rooted in a relationship to place and all the life that shares it?

Where—we all found ourselves asking at the Congress—is the life of peace, the capacity for identification with one another and the future, the imaginative stream of erotic possibility? All of us who are finding it so difficult to feel at home in the world these days must confront the fact that violence and war have together become the cornerstone of the North's relationship to the South. For those of us in the North, they pervade our national dreams and our public culture. We must liberate a politics of resistance before they compose our identity. We must find the political will to act, as our sisters in the South Pacific so eloquently insisted. They told us in no uncertain terms that it makes little difference whether the big elephants of the North are making war or making love; the lush and varied grasses of the South continue to be trampled. We returned home from Vanuatu knowing that if we remain intellectual witnesses, academics whose primary role is to critique and denounce, then all we will have done is empower complacency. The act of love is the energy of noticing.

Lobbying For Progress On Comprehensive Test Ban Treaty

Edna Ross

While the women at the International Pacific Policy Congress were meeting in Port Vila, Vanuata, the Partial Test Ban Treaty Amendment Conference was being held in New York. The stated aim of this Conference, called for by forty states frustrated about the lack of progress on a Comprehensive Test Ban, was to turn the Partial Test Ban Treaty (PTBT) into a Comprehensive Test Ban Treaty (CTBT).

On Friday, 11th January, six women from our conference paid a visit to Four High Commissioners at Port Vila, urging them to support the amendment for turning the PTBT into a CTBT. The delegation of women consisted of Rosalie Bertell (Canada), Lenora Foerstel (USA), Mal Johnson (USA), Marilyn Waring (New Zealand), Jean McLean (Australia), and Edna Ross (Australia).

The first call was to the British High Commissioner, Mr. John Thomson, who had prepared himself for our visit by reading the just arrived, latest update on British policy. Unfortunately, the change in world events over the last year was not reflected by any changes in the British position. There was nothing new in this policy. The British Government sees a comprehensive test ban (CTB) as a long term goal which is precluded for the present by the "problem of verification" and the continuing necessity of deterrence for British security. The British government believes that nuclear weapons have prevented a world war for forty years and feels that all countries would have to give up testing at the same time.

Our delegation argued that verification is now technically possible for all explosions down to one kiloton and that it was difficult to identify or prove that an "enemy" has been "deterred," for the deterrence theory must presume that an enemy wants war at all times as a matter of policy and this just does not seem to be the case. Furthermore, we pointed out that more people have been killed in wars in the last forty years than in all wars up to and including World War II. One could not say that this has been a time of peace. These arguments did not have any visible effect on Mr. Thomson, except to make him more defensive.

The delegation asked him to convey our request to his Government's representatives in New York that his Government not veto the proposal for a CTB. We left him with information on nuclear tests and on the history of negotiations to achieve a CTB.

Our next visit was to the High Commissioner from New Zealand, Ms. Carolyn Forsythe. We asked that our support for her Government's intention to vote for a CTB and our request that it protest all tests (not only French ones) be conveyed. The delegation also asked that the New Zealand Government be asked to call for a further amendment conference when the present one fails and that it intervene at the United Nations on the question of verification, pointing to the fact that it is now possible to verify explosions down to one kiloton. We stressed the need for the New Zealand Government to pursue the line that Johnston Atoll not be used for storage of chemical weapons and that no further weapons than the ones already committed be shipped there. Ms. Forsythe assured us that the New Zealand Government has taken Johnston Atoll seriously and intends to ensure that it is only used for what was originally intended.

The visit to the French Embassy, where we anticipated the greatest opposition to our messages, was amicable and excellent coffee was served. The Ambassador was not in Vanuatu and our meeting was therefore with Monsieur Charles Le Guern, the Cultural Affairs and Technical Cooperation attaché. Our request to the French Government was for it to set a date to end testing in the Pacific and for France to join a CTB. Monsieur Le Guern was not in a position to give such commitments, but listened to our case with interest. Monsieur Le Guern explained that the French Government's general policy is for a total ban on nuclear weapons; however, France's unwillingness to be under the umbrella of either superpower means they are committed to "nuclear defence" and testing until the two superpowers stop.

The economic and health costs of nuclear testing, the concern of Pacific nations regarding the effects of the French tests on the biosphere and the growing opposition, in France itself, to uranium mining and nuclear power plants were also discussed with Monsieur Le Guern.

Our last call was the Australian High Commissioner to Vanuatu, Mr. David Ambrose. Over Japanese tea, the delegation informed Mr. Ambrose about the PTBT Amendment Conference taking place in New York and asked him to convey our requests to his government in Canberra and then to its representatives in New York. Our requests included that Australia vote for a CTBT and not abstain; that it protest tests by all countries, not just French tests; that it call for another review when the current Conference fails; that it call for a reduction of the upper limit of explosions from 150 to 1 kiloton. As with the New Zealand High Commissioner, the delegation also discussed Johnston Atoll and possible Australian actions to ensure that an environmental impact statement is prepared.

As expected, the PTBT Amendment Conference in New York did not result in a CTBT. The amendment was not put to a vote because the United States and United Kingdom would have vetoed the amendment if a vote had been called.

A statement released by the Australian Government on 18th February, however, suggests that some progress on verification was achieved and that constructive discussion of CTBT in the Ad Hoc Committee on a Nuclear Test Ban in the Conference on Disarmament in Geneva will continue this year.

Josephine Abaijah, Chairperson of the National Capital District Interim Commission (NCDIC) of Papua New Guinea (*foreground*) sitting next to Hilda Lini, member of Parliament, Port Vila, Vanuatu.

Tropical Deforestation

Hilda Lini

Deforestation is one of the major environmental issues worldwide. It is caused by different forms of exploitative activities designed by man, such as slash and burn agriculture, large development projects, or flooding caused by dams and logging operators.

In the Pacific, slash and burn agriculture has always been part of subsistence farming and continues to be practiced out of ignorance to the damage caused to the environment. Development projects such as cattle ranching have also been ongoing, causing deforestation in parts of the Pacific. Logging, however, has become a major industry in some Pacific island countries, mainly the Solomon Islands, Fiji, Papua New Guinea, New Caledonia, and Vanuatu. Logging is promoted

---

Editor's Note—Hilda Lini is a member of Parliament for Port Vila, Vanuatu. Ms. Lini is well known for her activism and is recognized as a leader among Pacific women. As editor of *Pacific Island Profile*, Ms. Lini places great emphasis on issues related to the environment, women, decolonization, and the economy. The article published here on tropical deforestation appeared in the first issue of *Pacific Island Profile* in July 1990. It is important to note that most magazines and newspapers in the Pacific are controlled by western males. The launching of an independent magazine by a Melanesian woman is a radical stride against imperialism. Vanuatu, formerly the New Hebrides, is a chain of seventy islands with a total population of about one hundred thousand people. On July 30, 1980 Vanuatu became officially independent. In 1984, Ms. Lini's brother, Walter Lini was elected Prime Minister.

by governments which believe they are making good use of their forests to strengthen their weak economies as well as insure profits for land owners. Re-forestation as provided for in logging policies often means planting a single species of tree for future commercial use. Such activity undermines the balance of the ecosystem provided by the tropical forests and such re-forestation will never restore the original ecosystem once it is destroyed.

At least two Pacific governments have now banned logging because they are aware of the vast resources destroyed by such activity and the effects on the entire environment. Papua New Guinea decided to freeze its forest industry at current levels and implement a two year ban on new logging permits. New Zealand announced a ban on the export of native timber, which covers logs, sawn timber, and woodchips—saying the government had moved decisively on an issue of major environmental concern.

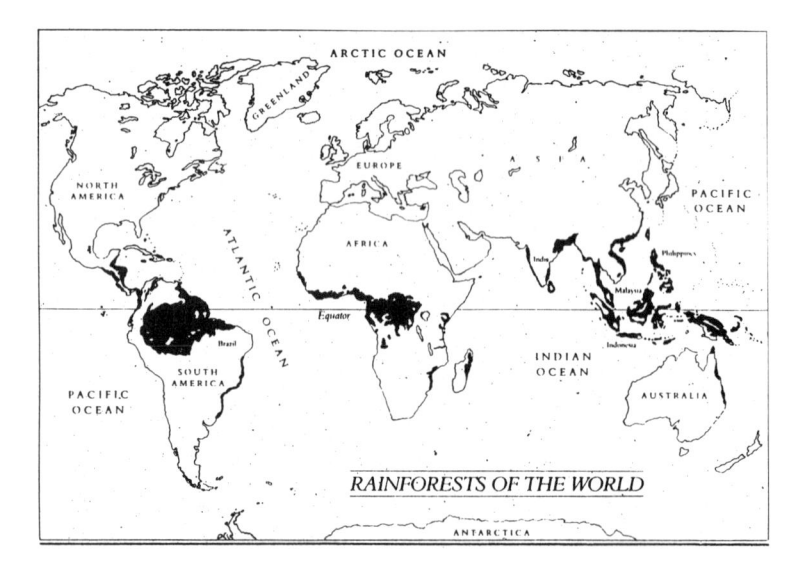

Rainforest Action Network

As this map shows, the South Pacific is home to some of the largest rainforests on earth. Each year 75 million acres of tropical rainforests are degraded or destoyed—144 acres every minute.

But how important is the tropical rain forest to the entire environment? According to the explanation provided in Awake! of March 22, 1990,

> As the name implies, rain is its outstanding feature. Over 20 centimeters may fall in a day, over 9 meters in a year. The rainforest is perfectly designed to cope with this torrential downpour. The canopy breaks the force of the droplets so that they cannot scour the earth away. Many leaves are equipped with elongated ends, or drip tips, that break up the heavy droplets. Thus the pelting rain is reduced to a steady dripping, which falls to the ground beneath with a softer impact allowing the water run off more quickly so that it can get back to transpiration. The cycle of water going from the atmosphere to the root systems accounts for ninety-five percent of the water that reaches the forest floor. As a whole, the forest absorbs rainfall like a gigantic sponge and then releases it slowly. When the forest is gone, the rain falls straight and hard on the exposed soil and eroding it off by the ton, ruining the land for farming or grazing.
>
> Effects on rain and weather patterns are even more disastrous. Rivers emerging from tropical rain forests are generally full year round. But without the forest to regulate the flow of water into the rivers, they overflow with sudden rains and then run dry. A cycle of floods and droughts emerges. Rain patterns may be affected for thousands of kilometers around, since a rain forest by transpiration contributes as much as half of the moisture in the local atmosphere.
>
> But deforestation may also affect the climate of the entire planet. Rain forests have been called the earth's 'green lung' because they draw carbon dioxide from the air and use the carbon to build trunks and limbs and bark. When a forest is burned down, all that carbon dioxide is dumped into the atmosphere. The excessive burning of carbon fuel may have already triggered a global warming trend called the

'greenhouse effect' which threatens to melt the planet's polar ice caps and raise sea levels.

As more awareness is raised throughout the communities, Pacific Islanders could take the lead in preserving forests.

Mining has an impact on the environment similar to logging. In the Pacific today, mining of various minerals is taking place in New Caledonia, Fiji, and Papua New Guinea. One of the major issues in mining is land, and it differs in a colonized situation such as New Caledonia and independent nations such as Fiji and Papua New Guinea. Whatever mining activity there is, in order to protect the natural environment the traditional landowner must insist upon a deal which would truly compensate for the destruction to his land and environment as well as a fair benefit from the profit.

The situation in Bougainville has been complicated by other forces, but originally Bougainvilleans have struggled long and hard against the way their environment had been treated. One entire village has been removed, valuable agricultural land destroyed, and the entire environment had been devastated to make way for mining. This open cut mining on Bougainville has created the biggest hole ever made by man in the world.

A study on the effects of mining at Missima in Papua New Guinea, which was conducted by the South Pacific Regional Environmental Programme, based in Nouméa, New Caledonia, is truly a lesson for the region.

While prospecting in the ocean and on land continues in the Pacific, island governments should be thankful that various mining issues have been highlighted by environmental activists for their future direction on mining activities.

Workshop—
Hidden From History:
An Examination Of Racism
Towards Aboriginal People

Leigh Bowden
Kaye Mundine

The group of women from around the world gathered in the meeting room. Everyone was asked to give their most vivid impression or image of Aborigines in Australia. For some, this related to first hand experience; for others it was merely images conveyed by the media in a range of forms. Knowledge of Aborigines by participants reinforced the conclusion that they had indeed been "hidden from history."

Kaye spoke about the label "black." She felt its harshness, and for her it included a range of expectations and attitudes that went with it. She spoke about access to knowledge and its equation with power. For Kaye and Aboriginal people in general being educated meant exposure to bullying, fear, and threat in spite of a love of learning inspired by her grandfather. Kaye had wanted to be a teacher, but this seemed an impossible goal for an Aboriginal girl. Her response was not anger, but to question "why"? Aboriginal society did not discuss these issues, but kept them on a personal level. Kaye's grandfather encouraged discussion. He kept the "spark" alive.

Kaye spoke of her childhood experiences. The Welfare Officer,

Kaye Mundine is a member of the Bundjalong Nation in New South Wales. She is an elected member of one of seventeen regional councils established under the Aboriginal and Torres Strait Islander Commission.

Leigh Bowden is a member of Action for World Development, Sydney, Australia.

in a cattle truck, would come to "save" the children to be civilized. Her grandmother made them all run away to the bush and hide.

Many of Kaye's childhood friends are dead. The "civilizing" process in welfare homes had "farmed out" many girls to work on properties. They often had babies. Legislation against this practice is still not in operation. Homesteaders still ask for girls to be sent as "housekeepers" to run all-male establishments.

While massive documentation exists, many Australians still know little about Aborigines. There is group resistance against investigating and learning about what is happening to Aboriginal people, particularly in the "deep north." Federal investigation of the treatment of Aborigines in Queensland was challenged by the state government. After the Royal Commission into Aboriginal Deaths in Custody won the case for access to records, those seeking information were told that the documents no longer existed. These records are not only historical but are linked to individual identities. Punishment was meted out to people who worked for Aborigines and also their families. People disappeared and the records can help them know who they are.

There is no longer such a phenomenon as "traditional people" —traditional life is now a museum culture; it is a stagnant concept. But cultural practices still thrive, even in urban situations. Sometimes, the practitioners are not even sure of the basis of the customs. But it is a myth that the culture and customs are lost. There is diversity among Aborigines as in any group. Aboriginality is not synonymous with homogeneity.

For Aborigines the question is not one of racism but of survival as human beings. Living conditions in some areas can be equated with the fringe-dwellers of Soweto. People are treated as rubbish.

There are no treaties between the white settlers and Aborigines because Australia was regarded as uninhabited by the British. Economics is the key to ownership of the land. Self-reliance had to be paramount for non-indigenous people who did not trust what the land offered and brought plants and so on from the outside. When Aborigines objected to water being contaminated by white bathing, they would be shot or poisoned. We still hear the cries of these people. Round-ups were seen as protecting Aborigines. In fact, this allowed land to be opened up to farmers. Then Aboriginal people were sent to work on these farms. Much of the labor was unpaid.

Land Rights Acts have given some little land to Aborigines. But among Australians there seems to be more interest in recruiting Aborigines to lend their voices to the movement against the Japanese buying land.

One New South Wales community has resisted relocation for generations. They felt they needed an economic base. They asked a Melbourne lawyer to buy the property on their behalf. This is still disputed as a legitimate practice by some. Other examples reinforce the resistance to Aborigines purchasing land.

In 1988, the Human Rights Commission called a hearing, known as the Tunia Enquiry. It involved about 500 Aboriginal people living at the junction of two rivers that were liable to flooding. Evidence was taken by video camera, as lawyers feared a loss of business if it became known they were defending Aborigines. What are the implications of this practice for justice?

Aboriginal people want things done now but the bottom line is that non-indigenous Australians don't want to acknowledge that Aborigines exist.

Kaye urged participants to:

1. Acknowledge Aborigines' existence,
2. Communicate with them. Communication must be approached from both sides. Aborigines need a sense of identity which comes from a recognition that they exist.
3. Consider the question of guilt. You are guilty until you do something about it!

Action for World Development (AWD) became involved in anti-racism work in 1987. A number of members observed a program to combat racism for and by non-indigenous people in Aotearoa and brought the principles back to Australia. They were then worked out in an Australian context.

Leigh showed the pamphlets used to advertise the program and the principles that have been developed for working in solidarity with Aboriginal people.

In the racism workshops, participants are encouraged to examine their colonial heritage and to see how they still benefit from the structures put in place by our non-indigenous ancestors. These structures were imposed upon indigenous people without their having any say or choice.

One key issue is the acknowledgment of the prior ownership of the land by Aboriginal people. All workshops begin with such an acknowledgment.

Action for World Development attempts to be accountable to Aboriginal people in its anti-racism work. Aboriginal monitors are invited to monitor each workshop and point out to facilitators any expression of racism that facilitators allow to go unchallenged. The monitors sit outside the circle while non-Aboriginal people examine their own racism. They are not there to provide information or answers or to justify themselves in any way. Facilitators and monitors meet after each workshop to discuss how the process might be improved.

Aborigines are only one percent of the Australian population. It is not possible for every Australian to have the opportunity to hear the Aboriginal story by speaking with an Aborigine. But AWD encourages non-Aboriginal people to seek out videos and books produced by Aborigines and to listen to what Aborigines are saying.

AWD defines racism as a combination of prejudice and power. The aim of the work is to bring about in non-indigenous people a change in attitude and a shift in power.

Leigh outlined the variety of workshops offered, ranging from a three hour simulation game to two-day workshops. By the end of all workshops, it is hoped that participants will have contracted to do something to change their own behavior. The aim of the workshops is to foster justice, not guilt.

At the conclusion of the workshop, all the participants agreed to the following resolution: <u>Challenge any ideas, thoughts, and words of racism and reject structures that foster racism. Challenge stereotyping and encourage people to accept diversity and that we are all human beings.</u>

Intercultural Collaboration In The Pacific

La Donna Harris

As an indigenous American, I would like to join my other American sisters in Women for Mutual Security in expressing our conviction that Pacific policy recommendations must follow on from a clear understanding of the psychological violence being experienced by the indigenous cultures of the region.

It is only after we have clearly articulated the implications of that colonial past and how the pattern continues on in the present that we can develop a more genuine form of intercultural collaboration that will be capable of reaching enduring solutions to Pacific policy issues.

Editor's Note—La Donna Harris rose out of Comanche culture, which made her particularly sensitive to the struggles of Native Americans. Recognizing the need for a national Naive American organization, she founded the Americans for Indian Opportunity in 1970. AIO is a national advocacy organization dedicated to the achievement of self-determination for all "tribal" peoples. Its major contributions have been in the areas of natural resource development, the development of the economies of reservations, and the enhancement of "tribal" self-government.

Ms. Harris has served several Presidential commissions, including the Commission on Mental Health and the National Council on Indian Opportunity. In the 1960s she helped to create the Citizens' Party and ran as a Vice Presidential candidate with Barry Commoner.

La Donna Harris (*left*) with Lenora Foerstel

Two different culturally-based patterns of decision-making underlie the nuclear and environmental issues we are trying to address. In the indigenous cultures of the Pacific, group identity is strong, collective ownership is valued, and decision-making derives from a process of consensus.

In the Euro-American cultures, on the other hand, individual identity is strong, individual ownership is unquestioned, and non-participatory representative government is the accepted pattern of decision-making.

While both value systems co-exist in today's Pacific, official decisions on policy issues are made without any viable linkage to the collective opinions of the indigenous culture groups. No forum exists for expressing such consensus-based points of view. It is not surprising, then, that Pacific policy issues still reflect Euro-American viewpoints or that their self-perpetuating, decision-making processes still dominate in the region.

But what of the indigenous viewpoints rooted in an intimate knowledge of the region's ecosystem and centuries of experience in successfully managing the region's resources? Should not the indigenous cultures be playing the key role in resolving the current debate on nuclear testing and toxic waste management for the region? Would not their culturally-based group identity and its sensitivity to the welfare of ensuing generations deny any use of nuclear power or any dumping of waste in the region?

This is the challenge facing us as women of peace in the Pacific region. In this, our first attempt to make a difference, we need to find a way not only to understand the collective viewpoint of the indigenous cultures, but also to make it part of collaborative decision-making on an ongoing basis.

How can we best nurture the articulation of such collective viewpoints? And how can we encourage collaboration that incorporates these collective viewpoints into wider multi-lateral decision-making processes? Let us bind together, as women committed to world peace and common security and devote ourselves to understanding the violence that past history has imposed on indigenous cultures and then to ensuring that indigenous Pacific cultures share as equal partners in regional policy decisions, knowing that sound principles for the protection of the region's environment and strong commitment to the sustainable development of its resources will inevitably follow.

(L - R) Annelise Droyer, Wenche Cumming, and Jacqueline Wasilewski

Workshop: Tribal Societies In Contemporary Times

Conducted by La Donna Harris and Jacqueline Wasilewski

Our group first struggled with the terminology of the session itself —the word "tribe." To some it connotes savageness and primitiveness, while alternatives, like "indigenous," still smack of colonialism. In any case, all the commonly used words are outsiders' classifications. The people don't refer to themselves this way. We never did resolve the issue of how outsiders should refer to native peoples, but for the purposes of this report, we will use the term "people of the land." Some of the ideas that emerged in this session were the following:

Large bureaucratic societal forms seem to be collapsing around us. Perhaps the remaining small societies of the world have valuable insights regarding the organization of human communities. In many of the world's hot spots, people are crying out for autonomy. Many of the things we have talked about in our conference, whether political or environmental, involve a lack of valuing on the part of these large bureaucratic social machines.

The struggles of the peoples of the land all over the world for autonomy, for the perseverance of their cultures, within the larger systems of which they are a part should be celebrated. Not only are there lessons of perseverance to be shared but these societal forms and their small governing units have insights to share regarding participation in decision-making and shared responsibility.

In these societies, being a good relative by treating all of creation —human and non-human, animate and inanimate—as kin is a key concept, a core value. Being in relationship generates belongingness, connectedness, a sense of who you are, that you are of value, that you do fit in, that you have a place. This kind of "identity" enables you to be "rooted" and "global" simultaneously.

Being in relationship generates certain behavioral protocols, certain clusters of mutual, reciprocal responsibilities and obligations, depending on the relationship. Each entity in the relationship contributes to the relationship and, therefore, is of value. You don't have to take away from one person in order to increase the value of another. Between sisters, for instance, the younger have the responsibility of physically taking care of the elder, of helping them. The older have the responsibility of nurturing the younger. Both have the responsibility of respecting the relationship, whether in an state of agreement or disagreement.

The point of many traditional ceremonies is to insure that life, that "the people," continue. Humans, thus, in a sense co-create the universe. Many peoples of the land create societies in which "the people" all come along together. How do we do this for the entire human community?

When there have been wrongs between us how do we proceed to get beyond blame, guilt, and shame. Getting caught in cycles of blame and guilt makes everyone victims. How can we communicate to others our pain without getting caught in cycles of blame? Our Maori sister said Maoris jump up and sing when the pain is overwhelming.

How do we have equal input into world development? How, for instance, can even the Peace Movement effectively listen to the peoples of the land, to the small societies in the world, to "the mice as well as the elephants" as our sister from the Cook Islands said, to the humming birds as well as the bears? The whole area of Peace Studies, for instance, began very conservatively and very small, with arms control and has moved through human rights and relational education. Ecology began and continues in some cases to be anti-human, putting nature above humans. We have to constantly be aware of the subtlety of dominance, of cultural imperialism, of institutional racism.

In the end, it was very difficult for us to put our discussion in terms of a resolution for action. A main stumbling block was the conceptual distance, for instance, between what even the word "relationship" connotes in the societies of peoples of the land and what that word connotes in the dominator's system.

Mexican-American Women Meet With South Pacific Women

**Lilia S. Velasquez
Juana Ventura**

This Congress brought to our attention the problems that effect South Pacific Women and their communities. It gave us a sense of connection and perspective as to the struggles experienced by South Pacific Island nations and reinforced our belief that the world community must unite and strive harder to find better ways to deal with the environmental problems that are depleting national resources worldwide. We were particularly impressed with Fanaura Kingstone. Fanaura spoke of the unbalanced relationship between the Pacific Islands and what she called the "Big Elephants" (France, Australia, and the United States), which continue to assert their influence in shaping and controlling the future of the Pacific. She recognized the importance of this conference because it provided the appropriate forum for Pacific women to voice their opinions concerning the ethnocentric attitudes that dominating countries have toward Pacific peoples. Fanaura stated that contrary to the beliefs of Western governments, the islands were always and are fully capable of deciding themselves on the development and preservation of their lands and future of their peoples.

It is important to understand the diversity of issues that we face irrespective of the countries we came from. And, equally important is understanding the common aspects of our struggles as we work together to preserve the earth.

As Mexican-American women from the United States, it was difficult to witness the prevalence and severity of the exploitive interference of our government in so many other nations. We observed the need to impart to our Pacific Sisters a greater awareness of the limitations of power that women's groups, even in the dominating countries such as the United States, have in influencing national policy. However, this realization should not dissuade us in our efforts to demand accountability from the governments of the U.S. and other dominating countries. We must stand together as women, irrespective of our nationalities, in order to draw upon the collective strength and support necessary to continue in our effort.

The Congress consisted of lectures and workshops. The lectures provided us with information regarding important issues such as

(L - R) Leslie Scott, Mal Johnson, and Lilia Valasquez.

hazardous waste dumping, racism towards indigenous peoples, and the nuclear armaments. The lectures were not just presentations of abstract theories and statistics but also focused on particular issues. The presentations stimulated in-depth discussions of the problems and proposed solutions by the participants.

The purpose of the workshops was to brainstorm the issues that were raised and come up with resolutions to present to the workshop leaders for subsequent discussion and approval by all Congress participants. An advantage to having an international group is that it allowed the representatives from various countries to discuss the solutions being utilized in their particular countries, thus giving us a wider scope of solutions, their probability for success, and the realities confronted in their implementation.

One of the highlights of the Congress was the invitation by Hilda Lini to attend a peace prayer and "teach-in" held locally at the Anglican Church. It was refreshing and inspiring to see people of all ages (including a large number of children) involved and interested to know the reasons why the United States and the allies it collected wanted to go to war against a tiny country like Iraq. After the peace prayer, we had the opportunity to embrace and talk to many of the people in the church. It was a touching moment to feel so welcomed in their community and to share with them our international concern for world peace; for a moment, cultural barriers ceased and we felt we were part of the community. It was impressive and inspiring to experience first hand the strong commitment of the South Pacific women in their efforts to educate people and work within their systems to bring about changes that enhance the lives of the women and children and thus ensure the survival of their culture.

Perhaps equally important was the opportunity for us to get to know our sisters here at home, in the United States, and the progressive work that they are doing in their communities and across the nations. We want to thank La Donna, Madeline, Leslie, Diane, and Jackie for their friendship and inspiration. For Juana and me, who are new to the Congress, the meetings were a great source of information and a good motivator to get us actively involved in peace and environmental movements in our home communities.

A lecture at the Pacific Policy Congress.

Workshop—
Australia In The Pacific: A Big Brother, A Stooge Of America, Or A Friend And Ally?

Dorothy Buckland-Fuller

I attended the Pacific Policy Congress because I am concerned about Australia's policies not only in the Pacific but in the whole world. I did not want to talk exclusively about "my" perception of Australia's present role in the Pacific; rather, I wanted to see what views of Australia would be put forward by other women in the Pacific, particularly non-Australians. We were scheduled for a two-hour workshop. I wanted to present my global philosophy and then listen to the way in which others see Australia and the role they would like Australia to play in the Pacific, so that I can take all this information back to the organizations I belong to and through them to our Government, in the hope that they too will "listen."

I have lived in Australia for thirty years. I teach, I am a mother, I am first and foremost a human being. I believe in the interconnectedness of the whole universe and I am concerned because I believe that everything we do in this or that country is going to influence eventually what happens in many other countries.

I am concerned about the Pacific, the Middle East, the military "industry," the destruction of the environment. Last year there was an Australian Arms Exhibition in Canberra; Australia selling arms to the world! I must say that in Australia we have a large number of people who are concerned about politics, women in particular in women's organizations. They care a great deal and are working towards a just and peaceful society—and a just and peaceful world.

Our world is shrinking; whatever happens in one country influences others. Aggression towards me, by individuals or governments, could extend to you one day and vice versa. We learn to be aggressive just as we learn to be loving. I have developed a philosophy of life which is based on "agape" in the Greek sense of the word which means "caring." I try to become more open and straight with people —no double talk. By opening myself, people open themselves to me so we can communicate better. I also try to learn more because knowledge is power. So I keep educating myself. This is my self development.

I am also a teacher, so I work at that level too. I tell my students that all I can do is open windows in their brain, round and round, so that they have a global view of the world and not a tunnel vision.

I work with networks. I am a member of a great number of organizations and committees and work within these networks to disseminate the information I get from one group to the other. I see myself as a catalyst and as a bridge. My activities aim at uniting and not dividing people. I use the telephone a lot. I phone a few people, they phone others, the information is passed on. Finally, I lobby politicians, individually and through the organizations I belong to. And, I call a spade a spade.

This is my way of living and working. What I plan to do when I return home is to pass the information I get from this Congress to all the groups and organizations I belong to. I am particularly keen to take back your ideas about the way Australia is going: is Australia going to develop as another Big Brother, like America? Is Australia to remain a stooge of America, as I see it, and I may be wrong. I speak from my own point of view. I also try to analyze why we are in this situation. Why people say that we have become a Stooge and when America says sneeze, we sneeze, or rather we catch cold.

Why are we in the Middle East?

To what extent has our government the right to interfere in other countries' affairs? What right have we got, when our own country is not in order?

All the problems you experience in your countries are present in ours too. Our children are suffering, our older people, the Aborigines, the ethnic communities, women. We have a class system. At the top are the upper class, highly conservative, male, middle aged Anglo-Saxons and at the bottom the Aborigines. Our "Labor" Government has lost touch with the needs and feelings or ordinary people. (I appreciate all the work the left wing of the Labor party is doing to bring about a more just and peaceful society). I too work for a just society. I have struggled all my life for justice for all peoples.

This is who I am. So you know where you stand with me. Now I would like to ask for your trust: to tell me how you see Australia? How you perceive us right now? Then we can go on together and develop an image of Australia, how Australia should be, as a "Big Sister" and not a "Big Brother." A Big Sister looks after everybody, a Big Brother bullies his sisters.

Maybe I am an idealist but, as a friend of mine used to say, we can't build a castle on the ground unless we first construct it in the air, that is in our mind's eye. I learned a lot from you. I share your worries and concerns. I care for you. I opened my heart to you. If you can open your heart to me, maybe together we can give a better world to our children. Black women say that white women do not "listen" to what black women have to say. Women of non-English speaking background, in Australia, say the same thing. So, for this workshop I decided to "listen." Now that I have presented my philosophy of life, my concerns, I want to devote the rest of the two hours allocated to the workshop "listening" and "noting" on butcher's paper what the Pacific women have to say about Australia and its role in the Pacific.

Perceptions of Australia:

There was much discussion on the following issues: aid, colonialism, social justice, Australia's statements on foreign policy often being different from practice, political ideals being undermined by economics and big business considerations, both Australia and New Zealand being used in the Pacific by the USA to set up a bulwark against the Russians in particular, Australia continuing to play this role by not pulling out of ANZUS as New Zealand did. The following is a list of what I jotted down as the Pacific women discussed Australia. It is both disturbing and encouraging. It is good to see that so many women understand the problems we face but it is also disenchanting to see such a long list of problems.

Surrogate for America
Hypocritical
Big Brother—bully
Setting itself up as the "regional policeman"
Opportunistic
Resources
Generous, but interfering—nosey
Immediate relief is improving
Racist—at home and in the Pacific
Anglo-European
Large white colonial country
Government is shackled—appeasement to big powers, media barons, and multi-nationals
Resources with strings
Missing the opportunity to identify itself as part of the Pacific, because of Anglo-European allegiances

Perception of "Ideal" Australian Role in the Pacific:

Responsibility to ensure that resources are shared
Accountability should be built in for aid and projects
Access of Pacific Islanders to education in Australia from High School onwards (open policy)
Be more culturally alert
Sensitive to needs

Seek needs before aid
Campaign at the organizational level for awareness of Pacific Nations and link up with Nuclear Free and Independent Pacific (NFIP) network to obtain more information
Australian government to do its utmost to deter all nations from nuclear testing and dumping of nuclear and chemical waste in the Pacific
Stop transportation of uranium
Stop Johnston Atoll incineration
Stop drift net fishing

Recommendations:

That Australia should be a friend and ally of the nations in the Pacific by being more culturally aware and sensitive to their needs and seek to understand these needs when offering aid. It should campaign at the organizational level for awareness of Pacific nations and link up with Nuclear Free Independent Pacific Network. The Australian Government should do its utmost to stop all nations' nuclear testing and dumping of nuclear and chemical waste in the Pacific. This includes transportation and incineration and chemical weapons on Johnston Atoll.

Appendix

Deforestation In Papua New Guinea

Mr. Gore: Mr. President, I would like to introduce a resolution today and tell my colleagues about it. Yesterday, I had an opportunity to meet with Justice Thomas Barnett, until recently of Papua New Guinea. The story he told was chilling. I rise today to introduce a resolution calling to the attention of my distinguished colleagues and the executive branch of our Government the trauma Justice Barnett has suffered and the tragic experience now underway for the people of Papua New Guinea.

I would also like to point out at this time that a resolution virtually identical to this one will be introduced next week in the European Parliament.

The story Justice Barnett tells is one rife with corruption, fraud, human rights abuse, and environmental devastation. Papua New Guinea is a small nation jutting into the South Pacific, and the home to some 3 million people. These are, for the most part, indigenous peoples, depending significantly on the forests of New Guinea, which constitute the largest remaining expanse of intact tropical rain forest in Asia. Yet, these forests are being destroyed so quickly that experts now fear they will be completely gone in less than 10 years. In their

---

Editor's Note—These remarks were made before the United States' Senate on March 21, 1991 by Senator Albert Gore, a Democrat from Tennessee. The text here is reprinted from the *Congressional Record*. We are grateful to Senator Gore for his remarks and his concern. See also the essay above by Hilda Lini on pages 112-116 above.

wake, these timber companies are leaving environmental devastation and human deprivation of the very worst kind.

Mr. President, the destruction of the rain forest is global. Over 40 percent of the world's tropical forests have already been destroyed. It is by now well known, I hope, that an additional football field size tract is being ripped out, ripped down, or burned down every second. In the process, the very threads of life are being severed.

Every 15 minutes, another species is lost. Some 100 species become extinct every day largely because of what is going on in the rain forests of the Earth.

In 1987, the Government of Papua New Guinea tried to act to stop the destruction. It was in that year that Justice Barnett began his own involvement and it is there when his story begins. He was given the charge by his Government of investigating forestry practices. He began to uncover severe abuses, illegal activities of the worst kind by the companies that were ravaging the rain forests. They were robbing the government of royalties, of export revenues, and of tax moneys, while cheating the indigenous peoples, robbing them of their homes, their culture, and the basic sustenance of their lives.

Justice Barnett discovered, for example, that the logging companies were making many tens of millions of dollars in profit, and yet, until 1986, not a single company declared any profit to the Government of Papua New Guinea.

Moreover, the companies were promising the indigenous peoples homes, money, and education in exchange for their land. What they delivered, however, was deprivation and destruction, forcing workers to labor in the forest seven days a week and under the most deplorable conditions. The companies in many cases paid them no royalties and in no case constructed for them the replacement communities that had been promised.

To the contrary, entire villages were bulldozed by companies eager to move logs. People were left in temporary shanty villages, sometimes on bare hillsides. Churches were destroyed, graves desecrated.

The companies would not tolerate resistance to their presence in the rain forest and harassed these indigenous lands into submission.

As Justice Barnett continued his official investigation, he discovered some high level government officials were deeply involved with the companies in their campaign of fraud and corruption. At this point, the enthusiasm for the investigation quickly vanished.

Justice Barnett's final report has been suppressed. Documents demonstrating the rampant corruption have been destroyed in fires, and Justice Barnett's life has been threatened. He was stabbed nearly fatally outside his home and has now been forced to leave Papua New Guinea.

The names of the companies primarily responsible for this destruction are familiar to us—the Nissho Iwai and Sumitomo companies are examples—continuing their pattern of destruction so evident in Indonesia and in Malaysia, especially Sarawak. These large Japanese companies are inflicting incredible harm on the indigenous peoples of the forest and on the living species that are being destroyed as the forests are torn down and burned.

The carnage must be stopped. In this resolution, among other things, I call on the Japanese Government to investigate the activities of these large companies and bring an end to their abuses.

Again, Mr. President, this resolution will also be introduced next week in the Japanese Diet.

But not only the Japanese bear responsibility for this tragedy, we, too, are involved, because while United States companies do not log Papua New Guinea, we are a huge market for tropical wood torn from similar forests.

I, therefore, urge my colleagues to join with me in calling for arrangements of technical and financial assistance enabling the people of the forest to survive and to stop the wanton destruction of the habitats of the many species that are being lost forever.

Mr. President, I will print the complete text of this resolution in the RECORD.

I might just say as a footnote, the coordinated action in the Japanese Diet and the European Parliament is being facilitated by the Global Legislators Organized for a Balanced Environment which is made up of legislators from countries around the world.

We have seen in several different locations of the tropics particular areas of rain forests that are singled out for intensive logging. Sarawak has been talked about quite a bit. The Amazon, of course, is probably the most famous example. Now Papua New Guinea has been singled out.

The ferocity of this onslaught is just devastating. This harm done, I have tried to note in these remarks, is so great that the world as a whole must speak out in an effort to stop this.

I hope, as a result, my colleagues will support this resolution.

Mr. President, I ask unanimous consent that the text of this joint resolution be printed in the RECORD.

There being no objection, the joint resolution was ordered printed in the RECORD, as follows:

S. J. Res. 101

Whereas the tropical forests of our planet are being destroyed at the rate of 40 to 50 million acres per year, often causing great damage to the environment, impairing ecological services, reducing biological diversity, impoverishing local communities and societies, and reducing resources for mankind's future;

Whereas this destruction, particularly in various nations of Southeast Asia, is closely connected to the logging and extraction of timber by Japan, the European Community and the United States; and whereas the largest remaining expanse of relatively intact tropical rain forest in Asia is on the island of New Guinea, biologically one of the richest areas of the Earth;

Whereas the Government of Papua New Guinea in 1987 commissioned an investigation under its Commission of Inquiry Into Aspects of the Timber Industry in that major timber-exporting nation;

Whereas the Commission of Inquiry produced a 20 volume, 6,000-page report detailing severe abuses and illegal activities by companies operating there, including defrauding the government of timber royalties, export duties and tax revenues through the practice of transfer pricing by virtually all large companies investigated; bribery of high-level government officials; violations of regulations intended to reduce damage caused by the construction of roads and the operation of logging; falsification of the species, quality, volume and value of exported timber, illegal logging; violating land rights and cheating landowners of proper royalties and benefits, and others;

Whereas the Commission of Inquiry concluded that the activities of timber companies in Papua New Guinea impaired the sovereignty of that country, and are major corrupting influences on the development of democracy in that emerging nation, having shattered the hopes and livelihoods of the poorest people in the country.

Whereas the findings of this Commission of Inquiry were not made public, nor have they formed the basis for criminal proceedings and other activities to ensure that illegal corporations are banned from logging and trading, and many corporations found to have broken laws still operate with impunity; and whereas only a few of the recommendations for needed reforms of the timber industry are being pursued, such as with the drafting of a new Forestry Bill, and the Government of Papua New Guinea has called upon the international community to provide necessary support to reform its forestry sector and has requested timber importing nations to restrain their demand for timber so as to not place an onerous and unmanageable burden on the timber resources of that country or exceed that nation's ability to manage its forests well;

Whereas the Papua New Guinea Commission of Inquiry provides a level of detail about the disturbing operations of timber companies participating in the international timber trade to a degree unlikely to be duplicated in any other country, and yet likely reflecting the nature of problems occurring in other timber exporting regions, and therefore should provide the basis for efforts to reform and control the international tropical timber trade and aid tropical forest nations to conserve their forests;

Whereas the creation of an international system to monitor international timber trade records and to authenticate the origin, species, and conditions of production of timber items would help ensure compliance with regulations, prevent illegal logging and profiteering, and would contribute to the preservation of forests;

Whereas timber companies should not be encouraged to pursue logging operations in primary tropical forests, as they have been found to operate frequently in violation of the most basic laws and regulations relating to income reporting and others, much less the more stringent regulations which would be needed to ensure that logging does not endanger the sustainability of forests ecosystems and their irreplaceable assets, such as biological diversity, and services to local communities.

Whereas a large proportion of the timber companies operating in Papua New Guinea are closely linked to companies headquartered in Japan, the largest timber importing country of the world, and a nation frequently criticized for the damaging effects of its timber consumption on the forests in various timber-exporting regions, most particularly Sarawak and Sabah states in Malaysia; and that Japan imports over 60 percent of logs exported from Papua New Guinea, and is involved in the trade of the bulk of the remainder;

Whereas the Commission of Inquiry found wrongdoing on the part of companies affiliated with companies based in Japan, and many in Japan are concerned about the use of that nation's Official Development Assistance (ODA) monies to fund roads, bridges, and other facilities for use by Japanesefunded corporations involved in the exploitation of Papua New Guinea's forests;

Whereas the fate of Papua New Guinea's forest resources and prospects for the proper administration of the international tropical timber trade depend on the recognition of the foregoing facts, and the urgent adoption of remedial actions. Now, therefore, be it

Resolved by the Senate and House of Representatives of the United States of America in Congress assembled, that the United States should call upon the government of Papua New Guinea to make available to interested parties the findings of, and take immediate action to implement the recommendations of, the Commission of Inquiry Into Aspects of the Forest Industry, and for the United States, though multilateral and bilateral aid arrangements, to provide technical and financial assistance to achieve these ends, including training, and strengthening the institutional capacities within the PNG government, educating landowners and providing funds for less-damaging extractive economies which preserve the environment;

That the United States should call upon the government of Japan to investigate the activities of certain of that country's private corporations and official aid agencies in violating laws and regulations in the conduct of their dealings in Papua New Guinea and in causing the destruction of the tropical forests; and to urgently seek the enactment of tax treaties and other arrangements with the governments of Papua New Guinea and other timber exporting countries to actively prohibit illegal activities and falsification of trade information; and to urgently work to reduce Japan's consumption of timber and to monitor and regulate its trade to ensure that all timber traded comes from sustainable sources;

That it should be the policy of the United States to call upon the International Tropical Timber Organization to create a system whereby all internationally traded timber is authenticated to ensure its true origin, species, volume, value and price, and to formulate and implement an urgent plan of action to ensure that all timber traded by the year 1994 comes only from sources managed without harm to the environment and societies in timber-exporting nations.

Louise Aitsi, Papua New Guinea

Participants of the International Pacific Policy Congress

Dorothy Buckland-Fuller
Individual Activist
New South Wales, Australia

Josephine M. Abaijah
Chairperson, National Capital
District Interim Commission
Papua New Guinea

Mal Johnson
Women for Meaningful Summits
Medialinx International
Washington, D.C., USA

Louise Aitsi
Papua New Guinea Activist
Papua New Guinea

Lenora Forestal
North American Coordinator
Women for Mutual Security
Columbia, MD, USA

Lloyd Edna Russel
Land Record Office
Vanuatu

Diana B. Sheridan
Associate Director, Center for the
Study of Women in Society
University of Oregon
Eugene, OR, USA

Amelia Rokotuivuna
Fijian Activist
Founder of the Nuclear Free
Independent Movement
Suva, Fiji

Janet Hase
Ministry of Education
Australian Teachers' Union
Teachers for Peace (Victoria)
Psychologists for the Prevention
of War (Victoria)
Hawthorn, Victoria, Australia

Juana Ventura
University of California San Diego
Bilingual Education
Habitat for Humanity
San Diego, CA, USA

Participants

Lilia Velasquez
Immigration Lawyer and Activist
Women for Mutual Security
San Diego, CA, USA

Hazel Tavoa
Port Vila, Vanuata

Kaye Mundine
Former Regional Director,
Queensland for the Human
Rights and Equal Opportunity
Commission Dickson—Australian
Capital Territory (ACT)
Australia

Joyce Clark
National Director, Australian
Peace Committee
Sydney, Australia

Pat Toms
Women's International League
for Peace and Freedom
President of the New South
Wales Branch
Potts Point, Australia

Duika Watson
Women's International League
for Peace and Freedom
West Hobart, Tasmania

Ngaire Teltira
Pacific Concerns Resource Centre
Auckland, New Zealand

Lyn Knorr
Williamstown, Victoria, Australia

Nitsuko Saito Fukunaga
Professor, Communications
International Christian University
Mitaka-shi, Tokyo, Japan

Madeline Duckles
Editor, Newsletter of Women's
Strike for Peace
Berkeley, CA, USA

Joyce Neave
Mullumbimby, New South Wales
Australia

Hansoz Matas
Port Vila, Vanuatu

Jean McLean
Member of Parliament
Victoria, Australia

Kuini Bavadra
Coalition Leader
Fiji Labour Party and
National Federation Party
Laitoka, Fiji

Annelise Droyer
Women for Peace
Norway

Ann Symonds
Parliament House
Macquarie Street
Sydney, Australia

Hettie Tinsley
Poet, Activist
Kensington South, Australia

Jacqueline H. Wasilewski
Assistant Professor, Intercultural Communications
International Christian University
Mitaka-shi, Tokyo, Japan

La Donna Harris
President, Americans for Indian Opportunity
Washington, D.C., USA

Leslie Scott
Coordinator, Peace Studies Program University of Oregon
Eugene, OR, USA

Hilda Lini
Member of Parliament
Port Vila, Vanuatu

Marie Muir
National President of the Union of Australian Women
Epping, New South Wales
Australia

Lorelle Savage
Coordinator, New South Wales Hidden from History Project
Action for World Development
Surry Hills, Australia

Delphine Willie
Vanuatu Police Headquarters
Port Vila, Vanuatu

Wench Cumming
Women for Peace
Norway

Mavis Robertson
Vice President, International Peace Bureau
Convener: Australian Coalition for Disarmament and Peace
Sydney South, Australia

Dr. Marilyn Waring
Feminist Economics Professor,
Department of Politics
University of Waikato
Aotearoa, New Zealand

Marie-Thérèse Danielsson
Women's International League for Peace and Freedom (WILPF)
Tahiti, French Polynesia

Susanna Ounei-Small
Presidente du Groupa des Femmes Kanak en Lutte
New Caledonia (Kanaky)

John Otranto-Semmler
Munich, Germany

Nadia Kanegai
Radisson Royal Hotel
Vanuatu

Rosalie Bertell
President, International Institute for Concern for Public Health
Toronto, Ontario, Canada

Leigh Bowden
The Ideas Centre, Action for World Development
Sydney, Australia

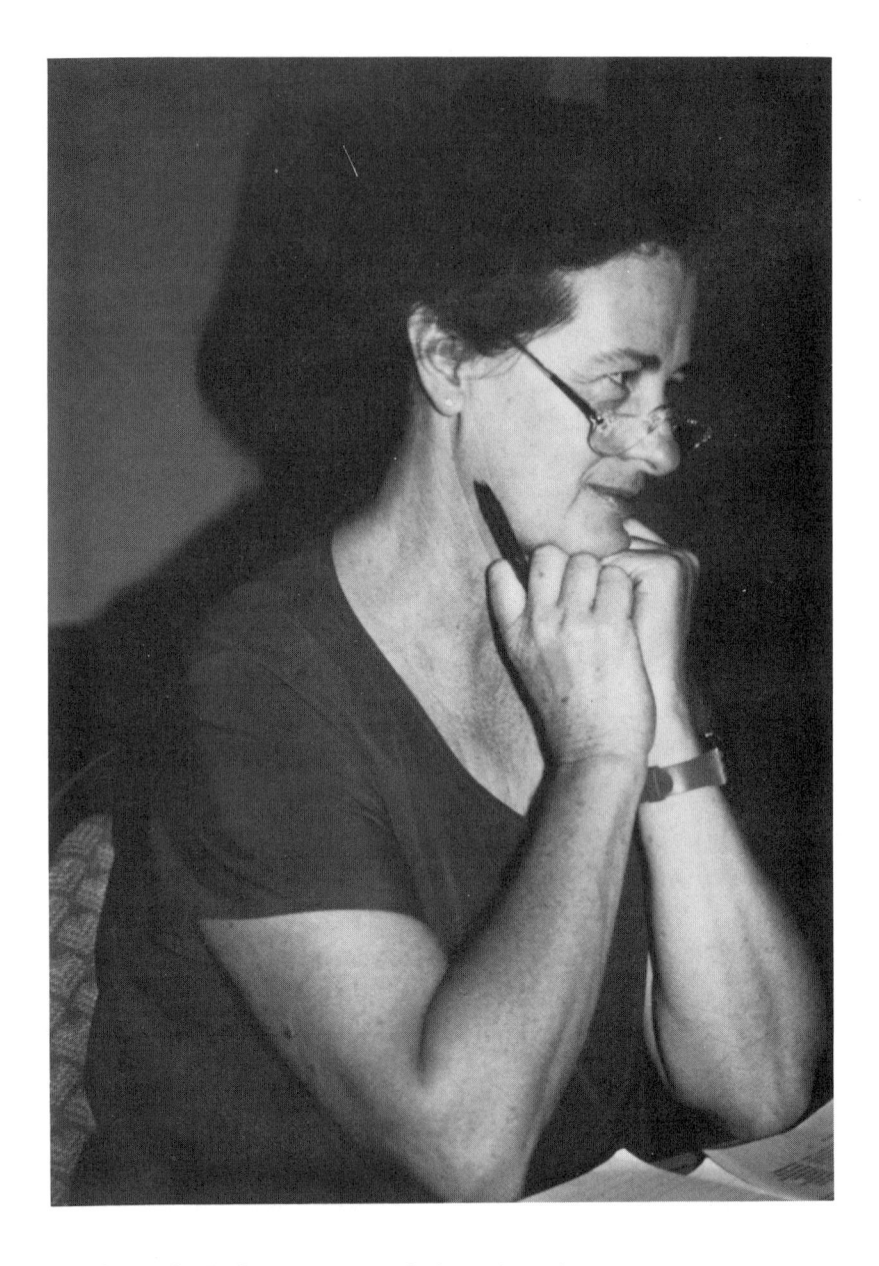

Ann Symonds, Parliament House, Sydney, Australia

Hilda Lini (*l*) and Pastor Allan Nafuki (*r*)

156 – Participants

Edna Ross
People for Nuclear Disarmament
New South Wales, Australia

Fanaura Kingstone
Social Development Advisor
Pacific Operations Centre
Port Vila, Vanuatu
(Citizen of Cook Islands)

Adi Kuini Bavadra (*l*) and Amelia Rokotuivuna (*r*)